THE SECRET INGREDIENT

THE SECRET INGREDIENT

Recipes for Success in Business and Life

GIGI BUTLER

Founder of Gigi's Cupcakes

with BUD SCHAETZLE

HOWARD BOOKS

New York   London   Toronto   Sydney   New Delhi

An Imprint of Simon & Schuster, Inc.
1230 Avenue of the Americas
New York, NY 10020

First Howard Books hardcover edition December 2018

HOWARD and colophon are trademarks of Simon & Schuster, Inc.

For information about special discounts for bulk purchases, please contact Simon & Schuster Special Sales at 1-866-506-1949 or business@simonandschuster.com.

The Simon & Schuster Speakers Bureau can bring authors to your live event. For more information or to book an event, contact the Simon & Schuster Speakers Bureau at 1-866-248-3049 or visit our website at www.simonspeakers.com.

Photos courtesy of the Butler family

Design by Jaime Putorti

Manufactured in the United States of America

The Gigi's Cupcakes logo is a registered trademark of Gigi's Cupcakes, LLC.

10 9 8 7 6 5 4 3 2 1

Library of Congress Cataloging-in-Publication Data

Names: Butler, Gigi, 1970– author. | Schaetzle, Bud, author.
Title: The secret ingredient : recipes for success in business and life / by Gigi
    Butler, founder of Gigi's Cupcakes, with Bud Schaetzle.
Description: New York, NY : Howard Books, 2018. | Includes index.
Identifiers: LCCN 2018021061 (print) | LCCN 2018021741 (ebook)
Subjects: LCSH: Butler, Gigi, 1970– | Cooks—United States—Biography. | Gigi's
    Cupcakes (Nashville, Tenn.) | Businesspeople—United States—Biography. |
    Cupcakes. | LCGFT: Cookbooks.
Classification: LCC TX649.B88 (ebook) | LCC TX649.B88 A3 2018 (print) |
    DDC 641.5092 [B]—dc23
LC record available at https://lccn.loc.gov/2018021061.

ISBN 978-1-5011-7352-3
ISBN 978-1-5011-7354-7 (ebook)

For the spirit God gave us does not make us timid . . .
—2 TIMOTHY 1:7

Behind every beautiful thing
There's been some kind of pain.
—BOB DYLAN, "NOT DARK YET"

CONTENTS

FOREWORD

----

by Debbi Fields

*W*hen Gigi Butler asked me to contribute my two cents to her inspiring, true-life story, I told her that I would be honored. Throughout her life, Gigi has continued to create possibilities in spite of the odds, even when the road ahead seemed insurmountable. Reading this book unleashed so many memories of starting Mrs. Fields Cookies. While our products are different, our Recipes for Success require the same key ingredients:

* Passion
* Perfection
* Perseverance
* People

Passion is obvious and contagious when you love what you do!
Perfection means creating a product or a service that is market differentiable and provides purpose.

Perseverance means having the guts to bring your specialty to the marketplace, not giving up on your dreams, and tackling the challenges that can easily overwhelm a budding entrepreneur.

People are your conduit to everything! Treat everyone with goodness, care, and love.

As you will discover in these pages, Gigi has embodied this Recipe for Success. Even through hardships she encountered while she set her dreams in motion, she overcame challenges, innovated through failure, kept the faith when no one believed in her, and found the strength to go on, even when she was blinded by exhaustion. Hers is truly a sweet story of success.

The Secret Ingredient is a delectably delicious read that will jump-start your passion for discovering—and rediscovering—your dream. It's a timeless reminder to stand strong against obstacles both real and imagined, and instead, like Gigi, launch your dream with innovation, hope, and determination. And don't let fear hold you back. Never give up on yourself—or your dreams!

With Love, Debbi

Founder and Chief Cookie Lover

Mrs. Fields Cookies

THE SECRET INGREDIENT

BAPTISM BY FIRE . . . AND FLOUR

- - - - - - - - - - - - - - - - -

The First Gigi's Cupcakes

*I*n the predawn hours of Thursday, February 21, 2008, the day I opened my very first Gigi's Cupcakes store in downtown Nashville, I lay in bed alone, snuggled up in the fetal position in my grandmother's quilt, praying for the blessed relief of sleep.

I'd just been through the most stressful twenty-four hours of my life, and I knew in my bones the new day about to dawn would be even worse. My stomach was doing somersaults, I was light-headed, and I could feel a panic attack coming on. But sleep had stubbornly refused to come, and here I was, unable to relax, every muscle in my body tight as a drumhead, the gritty metallic taste of adrenaline in my mouth.

I stared at my bedside clock.

1:47. It seemed as if it had been stuck at 1:47 all night.

I closed my eyes and thought about how much I like poetry and parables and self-help phrases. It makes me feel good to slap a Post-it up on the fridge that says "You Can Do It." I'd read *Poor Richard's Almanac* and I knew Benjamin Franklin wrote, "A watched pot never boils." Here in the privacy of my own bedchamber I was coming to terms with that aggravating reality.

I tossed and turned, rearranged the pillows and blankets, and rolled over so I couldn't see the clock. Maybe I could mentally transport myself someplace else for a little while. Conjuring an image of orange and gold poppies blooming in the High Desert near my childhood home, I imagined leaning into a warm breeze, the heat of the Antelope Valley floor rising up through the soles of my feet. I lay still for as long as I could, breathing evenly, trying to release the tension from my arms and legs.

After what seemed like an eternity, I finally turned back over to check the clock.

1:49.

– – – – –

I should have slept like a log. Wednesday had worn me out. As my small team readied the first Gigi's Cupcakes for its opening, I began the day working my "regular job" cleaning houses for Gigi's Cleaning Company, which I'd founded in California as an ambitious fifteen-year-old.

I cleaned an apartment and a huge mansion in Belle Meade— the "Beverly Hills" of Music City. Toilets, showers, marble floors, ovens, and laundry rooms blurred together as I motored along on autopilot. At four o'clock I raced downtown to meet my plumber, who'd just finished outfitting the new store. Together we checked all the sinks, drains, water lines, and restrooms. I owed him $350, but as I wrote him a check I told him, "Don't cash that 'til Monday. I just made a deposit—you gotta wait for it to post." He looked at me a little funny. He knew I was teetering on the edge financially. My homegrown plan to step up from the housecleaning business into the retail cupcake business had raised quite a few eyebrows. Gigi's Cupcakes would literally make or break me.

After the plumber left, I looked around the store. At first glance, it didn't look like we'd be ready to open the next morning—it really didn't. I tried not to freak out, and I reminded myself that the biggest pieces of the puzzle were already in place. The paint was dry, light fixtures were shining on refrigerated cases and appliances, custom countertops were ready for action, there was a brand-new floor, and baking tools and ingredients were poised in my glistening new kitchen. I watched my gung ho father, Terry, putting tables and chairs together while my mother, Ann, dutifully orbited the cheery space dust-busting little spots here and there. All was clean white, soft pink, bright olive, gleaming glass, and chrome. I was thrilled and overwhelmed that my dream was about to become a reality—but I honestly couldn't believe I had gotten this far.

My old friend Ted, a "get 'er done" general contractor who had worked hand in glove with me to bring Gigi's to life, dropped by to wish me luck. He could see I was nervous, but he murmured some reassuring words and patted me on the back. He handed me an envelope and quietly said, "Remember, I'll tear this up if you marry me."

The matrimonial reference rang an alarm bell. I opened the envelope and saw Ted's final contractor's bill, which in all the craziness I'd kind of forgotten about. The bill was for $15,000, but it might as well have been $15 million, considering that after the plumber's check cleared I'd have only $33 in my checking account.

I'd already bought, begged, borrowed, and stolen just enough to open the 995-square-foot shop, and I wasn't quite sure yet how I was going to pay my employees, keep the lights on, and buy groceries. "Stepping out on faith" was a phrase long popular in my entrepreneurially minded family, and I had staked my entire future on this new project. I had a plan A, but I'd blissfully—maybe even willfully—ignored the need for a plan B.

Suddenly everything piled up, and all the pressures that had been building just flattened me. My vision seemed to narrow; I couldn't catch my breath. I started to feel woozy, tears began rolling down my cheeks, and finally I slumped to the floor at Ted's feet.

He bent down to check me. "Are you okay?"

"I don't have fifteen thousand dollars!"

Ted, my dad, and my mom just stood there, frozen. Nobody knew what to say.

I'd met Ted six or seven years before, when I was singing in a band, cleaning houses, and learning how to make my way in Nashville. He was a successful contractor with a beautiful home out in Leiper's Fork, a rural village on the historic Natchez Trace Parkway that was home to celebrities like Faith Hill and Tim McGraw, Nicole Kidman and Keith Urban, and the Judds. He was a popular, good-looking guy, and a favorite with various local ladies.

Ted and I became purely platonic friends, despite his best efforts to take it further. I came to his parties and he invited me everywhere because we enjoyed each other's company. He regularly assured me that one day he would win me over, but I always told him it would never happen. I'd learned I didn't want a sugar daddy. I wanted to earn my own way—even if it meant cleaning toilets for the rest of my life. But his pursuit became kind of a running gag. My friends and I always laughed it off, and Ted always seemed to be fully in on the joke.

Sometimes we'd visit projects he was working on, and I was always impressed by the quality of his work and his attention to detail. So in late 2007 I went to him and told him I was going to open a cupcake shop.

"Well, congratulations," he said. "I'll build it for you if you marry me."

I laughed. "I'm not going to marry you. But I'll hire you to build it."

"Okay, I'll build it. But at the end of this project I want to marry you."

It never occurred to me that he might be serious.

So we built out the store together. The building, which had been part of a take-out restaurant, was gutted and reimagined as a friendly, welcoming sweet shop. I went down to city hall and stood in line to get permits and approvals and variances and waivers, and was very proud of myself for successfully navigating the city and county bureaucracies. Ted took the lead laying it out, my dad helped me design the space, and then he and my mom came in from Texas to help me out. She brought a welcome supply of enthusiasm along.

"You're supposed to help your kids," she'd say. So I'd load her up with research and chores and errands. We made a good team.

A few weeks before the opening, I caught up with Ted. "How much do I actually owe you?"

He smiled. "We'll figure it out on the back end."

I got a little concerned.

Now, just hours before Gigi's was set to open, with his unusual offer hanging in the air, I could see Ted's pride was on the line. He helped me up off the floor and steered me to one of my shiny new tables.

"Ted," I began gently, "we've been over this many times. I'm very fond of you, I really am. But I'm sorry, I just can't marry you because I don't love you that way."

Ted was hurt, but he kept his composure. He adopted a very professional tone. "Okay. Then you owe me fifteen thousand dollars."

It felt like he was flexing his muscles, declaring in so many words, "Fine, I'll show you." It rankled me, but the whole situation was so weird I didn't know how to reply.

As we watched him go, my dad shook his head sadly, like I was making a big mistake. "He was just trying to do you a favor, you know."

"What's wrong with you?" I snapped. "I'm not trading my hand in marriage for free drywall! I'll pay the bill, Dad. I just need to figure out how."

My mom chirped, "God will provide!" But I was more than a little shaken.

My parents and I spent the next few hours mopping the floor, arranging the tables and chairs, double-checking our stockpile of ingredients, and testing and retesting the refrigerators and the oven and the pantry. As day gave way to night, we took a last look around and decided we were as ready as we'd ever be. Soon Gigi's would be open for business—a real, living, breathing company, its shelves stocked with goodies made with love and care, crafted from family recipes handed down through several generations. Tomorrow we'd find out once and for all if this crazy idea would pay off—or wind up being the biggest mistake of my life.

I went home and tried to eat some dinner, but I could barely get anything down. Desperate to calm myself, I flopped in a chair and tried to watch TV. I picked up a book. I put on some music. I tried taking a nice hot bath. Nothing worked.

The truth was I was terrified. I was keenly aware that I'd failed before. I'd chased other dreams and come up empty— and they had all been small-bore, minor-league failures, painful but certainly not fatal. This was different. This would be big, and it would roll out in public, writ large. If Gigi's Cupcakes tanked, it would certainly not be the kind of flameout that would go unnoticed. Not only would I lose everything— I'd borrowed more than $100,000 to start Gigi's—but the faith, money, energies, and reputations of other people who'd helped and believed in me would be squandered. It could leave a stain that would never go away, souring things for me far into the future.

Making matters even more confusing, I kept hearing a little voice in my head saying, "God's going to take care of you, God's going to take care of you." But I wasn't so sure. How exactly would He take care of me? By making my new venture a success? Or by letting it fail so I would learn another lesson about humility and patience?

After bouncing off the walls for a couple of hours, I finally found a mental strategy that owed a lot to my previous experiences in business: I reminded myself that all I could do was my best, and the rest was impossible to control. I decided to open the shop and make the best cupcakes I could. If it flopped, I'd still have my health. Everything would be okay. I'd pay off my debts by cleaning twice as many houses and saving twice as much money. I'd figure it out somehow.

I finally crawled into bed after midnight and flipped through my Bible for a few minutes. I tried to pray, but I couldn't organize my thoughts. I gave up, took a Tylenol PM, turned out the lights, and started staring at that blasted bedside clock.

– – – – –

At 4:00 a.m. my eyes snapped open. Miraculously, I'd stumbled into a few precious hours of sleep. I rolled out of bed, stretched, and felt a little better. I gave myself a pep talk as I pulled on my clothes and headed out to the car in the predawn gloom.

"You're going to go do this," I said out loud. "You're going to go bake great cupcakes and sell them to people who will love them and come back for more. That's what you're going to do today, because you are not a quitter."

I drove through the empty streets of Music City. It was gray and spooky and chilly, kind of like what a metropolis would look like if aliens came and took everyone away. I thought about my mom's cry of "God will provide," which actually seemed like a reasonable assumption: I figured if God could deliver the unbelieving Israelites out of bondage in Egypt and part the Red Sea, He could surely stiffen my spine and help get me through one high-stakes, red-letter day in little ol' Nashville, Tennessee. I had faith, and I reckoned that somehow we'd make it work together, God and me. I had been scared before, and He had helped me then. He'd be here for me again.

When I first saw *Indiana Jones and the Last Crusade* as a little girl, one scene really hit home. Indiana was on one side of a wide chasm, and on the other side was a vast treasure. To reach it, Indy had to step out across the chasm but he couldn't see a bridge: He had to have *faith* that there would be more steps beyond that would allow him to reach the other side. I thought it was a cool way to visualize your path forward. So whenever I'm really apprehensive about something, I remember that I must keep "stepping out on faith" and God will show me the path.

I had also been listening to Christian speaker Joyce Meyer, to how she embraces the concept in her own way: "God will tell you when you're not on the right path. He'll let you know. But until then, keep moving forward. Keep stepping out."

So there I was at five in the morning, "stepping out." I don't know that I actually prayed for a sign that God was watching over me, but as I headed into the city toward my new destiny, every single stoplight turned green. I went four straight miles through the heart of town on totally empty, green-lit streets. And as every light turned over from red I thought, "Hey, that's the way to start this day—green lights all the way!"

That morning I could feel God's strength. I thought, "Lord, you've prepared me for this. People told me I wasn't good enough, I didn't sing well enough, I wasn't pretty enough. But every rejection prepared me, made me stronger. And now, the lights are all green." I felt His hand on my back and heard His voice saying, "You can do this. Go. Go. Go."

I pulled up to Gigi's Cupcakes and took a moment to savor the sight. There it was, my name on the front door, a new adventure about to take flight. I wondered if the journey to this modest little parking lot wasn't really about more than just cupcakes. Could it have been an exercise in personal growth, in finally finding my truest compass heading? I was about to re-create myself and write a new chapter in the story of my life, and I knew that not everybody gets that kind of chance. Whatever was about to happen, I felt profound gratitude.

At 5:00 a.m. sharp, my little staff showed up. We were all excited and nervous. Sharon Sweat, Leah Parker, and David Johnson all looked to me for guidance, and I was trying to be a good boss. "All right, team. We got this. Today's the day!"

We went inside, turned on the lights, and spread out across the kitchen. Everything was new. Nothing had been used before. Now everything was about to change forever.

I pulled on my apron, a beautifully handmade "good luck" gift from my mom, who'd stitched delicate, colorful cupcakes across the front. It felt good having a piece of my family with me; it was almost as if I were slipping on a suit of armor.

"Fire up the ovens," I said. "Let's bake. Let's do Hunka Chunka Banana Love."

This was one of my most beloved recipes, one that never failed to get oohs and aahs at parties and family gatherings. It was a thick, rich, buttery banana bread that I gave to my house-cleaning clients every Christmas, a foolproof crowd-pleaser based on an old family recipe. It seemed like the perfect cupcake to launch my new venture. Everybody nodded—this was a no-brainer. We got out a big ol' bowl and started mixing it.

That first morning we baked a handful of recipes: Hunka Chunka Banana Love, Coconut, Scarlett's Red Velvet, Golden Brown (Grandma's Favorite Yellow Cake), Midnight Magic, and White Midnight Magic. We felt our way along about how much to mix, how much to bake, how many different flavors looked good in the cases, and what we thought people might respond to. We baked . . . and baked . . . and baked.

The sun came up, cars started whizzing down Broadway, the city came to life, and then suddenly it was 9:00 a.m.—time to open Gigi's for the first time.

I went to open the doors, but on the way I ducked around the corner. I didn't want anyone to see me as the tears came—tears of joy, tears of fear, tears of hope, tears of gratitude.

But I also felt a brief wave of panic: "What am I doing? What am I doing with my life?" I was suddenly shaking, ecstatic and petrified at the same time. After a minute or so I got hold of myself and thought, "We made it! We're opening!"

I unlocked the doors, and we sat there for thirty minutes, watching the clock. Just as I was starting to vibrate from the thought that this whole idea had been a wild miscalculation, our first customer walked in. I had the presence of mind to take a picture of her. She bought six cupcakes to take to a friend who was in the hospital. "These are for the nurses as much as they are for the patient," she confided sweetly, fully on top of how best to grease the wheels in a hospital ward. She paid in cash, and I tacked her five-dollar bill up on my little menu board, where it would hang for years. On her way out she winked and said, "Remember, I'm your first customer."

What an amazing morning it turned out to be. We weren't exactly swamped, but we had a steady stream of customers, and many were curious to find out what a "high-end" cupcake tasted like. They'd stop at the door and say, "Are you open?"

"Yeah, come on in!" I had fun talking with everyone, explaining the origins of my recipes, and watching people's faces light up when they took their first bites.

"Oh my gosh—this is the best cupcake I've ever tasted," said one young woman who came in with an apple-cheeked baby in a stroller. "It's not too sweet, but it's so creamy!"

Now, I'd always thought my cupcakes were pretty tasty, but I wasn't prepared to hear such glowing reviews right out of the box. It seemed we had struck a chord—and created something brand-new. Watching customers revel in the flavors and textures of my cupcakes was deeply gratifying, and it reminded me of what it had felt like to get a huge round of applause when I was performing onstage with my old band.

A little later in the morning, my mom and dad came in and worked the counter with us. They were so pleased and proud to see so many people enjoy my creations. At one point my dad leaned over and said, "Looks like you might be on to something here, kid."

We sold 253 cupcakes that first day, which was 253 more than some folks thought possible. We got through the day without any catastrophes. We didn't run out of anything critical, we didn't make any glaring mistakes, and when we closed the doors at the end of our first shift we looked at one another, breathed a collective sigh of relief, and started laughing. Most remarkably, a quick calculation told us we'd actually covered our costs for the day! We'd started off with a bang, and everybody was energized. As we headed home that first night, we agreed we were all looking forward to getting up and doing it all over again.

The next day was a Friday, and we sold 310 cupcakes. Customers told us they'd been hearing things from their friends like, "Wow, have you been to this cupcake shop called Gigi's? It's down on Broadway . . ."

We hadn't even really made any noise yet—we hadn't done any press or advertising, just a little social media. But over the next few weeks our clientele would just keep growing.

Before long, customers started tapping on the glass well before 9:00 a.m., and one morning Miss Sharon came to me and said, "Since we're here by five, we can bake and frost four or five different batches and have them out front by seven thirty instead of nine. We can open earlier and catch the morning crowd going to work."

I thought it was a great idea, and soon the downtown crowd was coming in to buy cupcakes to take to work. Pharmaceutical reps got wind of Gigi's and quickly became a big part of our business, buying dozens of cupcakes at a time, taking them to the hospitals and doctor's offices and giving them away. Turns out a cupcake is a really great tool to schmooze with.

The Vanderbilt University Medical Center community also got in on the act. Doctors, nurses, office workers, administrators, patients, and family members all dropped in for a little Gigi's, and they enthusiastically spread the word among their friends, clients, and patients. Now Vandy customers come in and say, "We're from out of town and when we come to Vanderbilt we always stop at Gigi's." It probably happens twenty times a day now. My favorite is when a little kid being treated at Vanderbilt comes in. The mom will say, "My daughter had a doctor's appointment and I wanted to make it special for her—so I told her if she was a good girl she could have a Gigi's cupcake."

Gigi's Cupcakes was off and running.

And as for that $15,000 bill? My mom was right. God did provide and I eventually paid it off in full.

– – – – – – – – – – –

Lessons for Life and Business

Step out on faith and go for it. Don't be afraid to take the leap. If you don't take chances, you don't win—period.

HUNKA CHUNKA BANANA LOVE

*T*his recipe has so much meaning. Not only was it the first cupcake I baked the morning I opened the original Gigi's store in Nashville, but I also made it for gifts every Christmas season. When I had my cleaning business I didn't have much money, but I wanted to show my clients my appreciation. I would bake these in little bread tins and tie them with a ribbon along with a card of Christmas blessings. Now this recipe has come full circle; it is available as a loaf in all our stores during the holidays.

INGREDIENTS

4 ripe bananas, mashed

2 cups sugar

4 large eggs, beaten

1 cup vegetable oil

2$\frac{1}{2}$ cups all-purpose flour

1$\frac{1}{2}$ teaspoons baking soda

1 teaspoon salt

1$\frac{1}{2}$ cups chopped pecans

1 cup dark chocolate chips

- Preheat the oven to 350°F. Grease 2 loaf pans or muffin tins.

- In a large bowl, hand mix the bananas, sugar, eggs, and oil until well blended.

- Add the flour, baking soda, and salt and mix until combined.

- Fold in the pecans and chocolate chips.

- Divide the batter evenly in the prepared pans or muffin tins.

- Bake for 25 to 35 minutes. (If using muffins tins, bake for 15 minutes.) If a toothpick comes out clean, they're done!

ROOTS

_____

A Wonderful, Maddening, Loving, and Crazy Family

I grew up in a godly and grounded home. Although my parents had plenty of ups and downs, they were good, decent people who taught, encouraged, and supported all their children. They both came from colorful families that prized honesty, hard work, and dignity.

Mom and Dad were both born during World War II. My mother, Shirley Ann Nodini, grew up half Italian and half Scots-Irish near Lawton, Oklahoma. My father, Terry Lee Butler, was from Gardena, California. He met Shirley in Altus, Oklahoma, when he was serving in the air force. After a whirlwind courtship, they married on June 27, 1964. After his air force hitch was up, Dad and his new bride returned to his native Southern California, where he had found a job at an electrical company. But before he could start work, the company owner died unexpectedly. It was a shock, and it left the young couple scrambling for a plan B.

There was a major butchers' strike under way in Los Angeles about this time, and Mom and Dad read in the papers how local meat processing plants were growing desperate at their inability to fill their orders. They drove downtown, crossed the picket line, and got themselves hired as meatpackers. Dad worked hard and impressed his bosses, who offered him a job at a Safeway in Lancaster, a town an hour away out in the High Desert. Soon Mom was working as a seamstress in a local fabric store, while Dad worked his way up the Safeway ladder. That first year, they couldn't even afford a Christmas tree; Mom scavenged a throwaway from one of the neighborhood tree lots.

After my father had worked five years at Safeway, my brother Steve was born, and Dad learned through his network of air force buddies that the Los Angeles County Fire Department was hiring, and that it was offering special preference to military veterans. It was more money, better benefits, and more excitement. It seemed like a good next step. He applied and got the job.

Mom was pregnant with me at the time, so they decided that while Dad was going through his intensive fire and paramedic training in L.A., she would go to her parents' farm outside Lawton, Oklahoma, where I was born on January 3. A massive snowstorm hit the day after New Year's, and I'm told the ride to the hospital was hair-raising. I came along at 9 pounds, 10 ounces, 22 inches, with a full head of dark hair, looking just like Jackie Gleason. The doctor reportedly said, "Why, she's big enough to go to school." Six months later, my dad had completed his training, and the Butler family headed off to start a new adventure in Quartz Hill, where my brother Randall was born.

It was always hot and windy in Quartz Hill, a desert community in the Antelope Valley, an hour north of Los Angeles, and there wasn't much culture. Whenever people say, "That's mean," I say, "You obviously haven't been to the Antelope Valley." There's a lot of military in the area, which doubles as a training site for U.S. forces who will be deployed to the Middle East. The army built mock Afghani villages up in the mountains, and I'm told that when our soldiers get to Afghanistan, the pictures they send back look like the Antelope Valley.

Living in the California High Desert was quite an experience. Many people love it, but just as many find it disheartening and desolate. There were more than a few things I found beautiful about the desert. I don't think you could find a prettier sunset. And the Antelope Valley grasslands come alive each spring with an unbelievable explosion of wildflowers—mostly richly colored poppies that draw tourists the way the Blue Ridge Mountains draw leaf peepers every fall. It's as if the desert floor is suddenly covered with red, orange, pink, and violet paint—quite a gorgeous display by Mother Nature.

And its unique landscape makes an impression that stays with you. When the *Apollo 11* guys were performing the first moonwalk in 1969, Neil Armstrong described the surface of the moon. He said, "It has a stark beauty all its own. It's like much of the High Desert of the United States . . . it's very pretty out here." Of course, Armstrong and his fellow astronauts and test pilots spent years out in the High Desert at Edwards Air Force Base, training and testing high performance aircraft. They knew the area as well as anyone, and it occupied a special place in their hearts.

Growing up in a place where the wind never stops blowing, I had a rough-and-ready life spent outdoors exploring and adventuring. Everyone was in 4-H and everyone spent time on farms. We played ball and went camping and canoeing. We cooked out under the stars and never stopped trying to keep the sand out of the house. Ours was a country town, and we loved it. We got our first stoplight in the 1990s, which replaced the stop sign on the corner by the drive-through dairy. We took pride in our tight little community.

Our neighborhood had been an almond orchard in the 1920s. The town's founding fathers discovered that despite the wind and the constant heat, if you watered something enough, it would grow. Oddly, out in the middle of a desert, a new planting would jump-start something deep in the soil. Things would just sort of magically bloom where they were planted. Eventually, this became a mantra for my mom. She would always say, "Remember, Gina, we all have the opportunity to bloom where we are planted."

We planted a huge garden with lots of different vegetables and raised chickens, geese, turkeys, ducks, pigs, and peacocks. I look back on it now—the fresh veggies, meat, and eggs—and I realize we were pretty much self-sufficient.

Our house was a fixer-upper, and I spent my first years crawling through sawdust as my dad finished one room after another. Terry Butler may be the most talented human being I've ever known—a self-taught mason, carpenter, electrician, butcher, plumber, canoe-maker, cabinet-builder, even a restaurateur. He could pretty much do anything he put his mind to. He wound up rebuilding our whole house, and then he rebuilt it again and again. Over twenty years he never stopped improving it.

He encouraged us to follow in his footsteps, to pick up new skills wherever we could. My brothers and I would load a wagon with eggs and vegetables from our farm and walk down the street selling them. We always had something going on.

Dad had an entrepreneurial spirit and was not afraid to try anything. He'd buy cars, fix them up, and resell them. One day he decided to get into the potbellied pig business, because Vietnamese potbellied pigs were a pretty big deal at the time. We got two potbellied pigs, and they multiplied into fourteen in about six months. Then the bottom fell out so we had potbellied pigs as pets. (The pigs were very smart, by the way.) After that it was turkeys. Then bunnies.

When I was fourteen, Dad decided to start a hair salon.

"Dad," I said, "we don't even cut hair. How's that going to work?"

But that didn't stop him. He also started an arcade in Palmdale and rented video games to convenience stores around Southern California. Once a week he would go from Barstow to Victorville to Canyon Country and back again, collecting quarters and fixing the game consoles.

He started a restaurant called the Snack Attack Café in the middle of town. My mom made cinnamon rolls every morning, and I waited tables and manned the cash register after school. The business didn't last long because Mom was busy and couldn't really run it on her own. So then Dad bought a Great Steak & Fry franchise. Business boomed, and we expanded to five locations. That went well for a couple of years; then he sold the franchises.

As all this was going on, Dad was working regular shifts as a paramedic engineer with the LACoFD up in Canyon Country, where he worked forest fires, accident scenes, riots, earthquakes, and freeways. He averaged about sixteen runs a day and really enjoyed this part of his career. I remember him saying to me that helping people would be the most satisfying thing I could ever do in my life.

Since I was growing up with this energetic entrepreneur, it was no surprise that at a tender age I started developing my own empire-building outlook!

— — — — —

My parents were always intent on broadening the horizons of their children. Their generation worked hard to make sure their kids had a better life than they did, and opening our little eyes to the wonders of the world was a critical component. Cultural experiences were the easiest way to pique our curiosity, so we were introduced to a steady diet of interesting food, music, theater, and other traditions. Above all, we *traveled*.

I may not have been raised in the heights of society, but our cross-country travels opened my eyes to the sights, sounds, accents, flavors, and textures of places like Arkansas, Colorado, Nevada, New Mexico, Mississippi, Texas, and Louisiana. By introducing my brothers and me to such richness, my parents taught us to appreciate the many facets of our wonderfully diverse nation.

When Mom would make something from one of the places we'd visited—Mississippi mud cake after a visit to Biloxi, for instance—a little piece of that culture would take root in each of us. She thought a good regional recipe was a fun way to expand our horizons. And, no surprise, I'm now encouraging my own daughter with the same tradition.

I think God gave us five senses to tell us how much He loves us. He wants us to use them to stay connected to one another in the here and now, but He also wants us to use them to remember where we came from, and to stay in touch with all the wondrous moments that lifted us up and drew us together. He seems to be saying, "I really love you and I really care for you—and I made you special in this way."

We always ate well. Mom was always there when we got home, ready with a hug and kiss, her kitchen overflowing with homemade cookies and pies. I realized that food—cooking it, serving it, eating it, sharing the experience—was a key part of the vocabulary of love between human beings—what my family called a "love language." And in our home, the dinner table has always been the modern-day version of a prairie campfire, a gathering place where we share our lives with those we love.

Even though we lived humbly, we always had just enough money to go on trips. Every summer we would pack up the truck—or a motor home if Dad had had a particularly good year—and travel around the country. Nineteen eighty was a motor home year, and one of our stops was in Ozark, Arkansas. We saw a "U pick 'em" blueberry place. My mom was in heaven. We stopped and picked about five gallons of blueberries that day. While we drove along, she canned blueberries, baked pies, made blueberry pancakes and muffins. We ate blueberries that entire summer. Blueberries are still my favorite food of all time. Whenever I make my blueberry cobbler recipe I am reminded of that summer.

----- ----- -----

We spent a part of each summer in Oklahoma with my mater-
nal grandparents, who lived on a dirt road outside the town of
Mountain Park, population 450, which had originally been a
trading post on the Kiowa, Comanche, and Apache Reserva-
tion. We would go up the slopes of the mountain to play every
day and soak up the history and lore of the area. The locals spun
plenty of yarns about cowboys and Indians and railroads and
U.S. marshals, and we ate it up.

My grandparents were generous and loving. But they'd been
through the Depression and never would buy anything they
could make themselves. They wanted us to be prepared to take
care of ourselves, so they taught us how to scrounge, scrimp,
and save. Grandpa had a ball of rubber bands that must have
been two feet across. It was so heavy I couldn't even pick it up.

I'd ask, "Why do you need this?"

"Just in case," Grandpa would answer.

I'd press him. "In case of what?"

"You got to be ready." He'd smile, as if I couldn't possibly
understand what it was like to have absolutely nothing.

And they'd can, pickle, make jam, grind corn, and bake.
We'd pick peaches by the Red River and can them for ice cream
and peach cobbler. This is where my peach cobbler recipe came
from.

As for my grandmother Edrie, she was adventurous and
had a restless spirit. She taught me so much about seeing the
world through wondrous eyes. When I was eight, she took my
brothers and me on a "Hostess run." We rode in her Cadillac
El Dorado up to Altus to the day-old Hostess outlet, and we
basically bought out the store. We sat in the backseat while

Grandma filled the trunk with cookies, Twinkies, Ding Dongs, Sno Balls, and Honey Buns. Once the trunk was full, she said, "Sit still, here comes the rest of the goodies." We literally had piles of Hostess goodness all around us. On the way home I looked over and saw Randall with a Honey Bun in one sticky little fist and a Twinkie in the other, taking alternating bites from each.

"This is heaven," he said as the sugar took hold. Psychologically, I'm pretty sure this helped jump-start and reinforce my love for baked goods; I could see how they made so many people happy!

When we got home, Grandma put all the baked goods in her freezer, and we ate Hostess products for about the next four summers. Sno Balls were my favorite, and once a year or so I'll pick some up at the grocery store, and I always think of my grandma.

My great-grandpa Jim Willis's mother, Rebecca, and her brothers had owned a bakery in Clinton, Oklahoma, called Bill's Bakery. Rebecca was a wizard baker, known for her elaborate, multilevel wedding cakes. When she died in 1913, she had firmly established a baking tradition in her family, which was dutifully handed down through the generations. Oklahoma is where my love for baking began as I knocked around the kitchen with my grandma, my aunts, and Mom. They taught me their "love languages," and I learned how to make breads, cookies, desserts, casseroles—all while standing on a stool and watching. I may not have gone to culinary school, but I certainly learned from the best. We'd turn peaches into pie, blueberries into muffins, and strawberries into tarts.

In retrospect, I guess I've never run across another family that reveled in entertaining and cooking and baking as much as my family did. Most of the women—Mom and her sisters, Bennie and Marie—studied home economics in school, could whip up a great meal out of nothing, and knew their way around a garden. My mom is a wealth of knowledge, a walking encyclopedia, a master gardener, and a touchstone for who I am.

When I was young, it seemed routine to have this kind of creative freedom and discovery. Nowadays, when kids are always running to soccer practice or studying for tests, they don't necessarily have time to just be kids—to create, to sing songs and hunt frogs and climb mountain slopes. But I had time to absorb my family's roots and traditions, and to reflect upon the larger world in general. Those summers were full of wonder, and they were some of the greatest gifts my parents ever gave me.

- - - - - - - - - - -

Lessons for Life and Business

Always be open to new beginnings and experiences. You never know what might be just around the bend.

BLUEBERRY COBBLER

*B*lueberries, as we have seen, are God's perfect food. 'Nuff said.

INGREDIENTS

10 cups fresh blueberries (or two 16-ounce bags frozen blueberries)

2¹/₂ cups plus ¹/₄ cup sugar

1 teaspoon lemon juice

1 teaspoon lemon zest

¹/₄ teaspoon salt

¹/₂ teaspoon vanilla extract

¹/₄ teaspoon ground cinnamon

2 tablespoons cornstarch

2 tablespoons all-purpose flour

Gigi's Piecrust (page 211)

3 tablespoons butter

- Preheat the oven to 375°F.

- In a large stockpot, heat the blueberries, 2½ cups sugar, lemon juice, lemon zest, salt, vanilla, cinnamon, and 3 cups water on medium heat and stir occasionally, until simmering.

- In a small bowl, combine the cornstarch, flour, and ½ cup water and whisk until blended. Add to the blueberry mixture and stir well. Let it cook until hot and bubbly. Remove from the heat.

- Make Gigi's Piecrust recipe. Roll out half the dough to fit into an ungreased 9 x 13-inch glass baking dish.

- Pour the blueberry mixture into the pie shell.

- Roll out the other half of the dough, cut into strips, and make a basket pattern on top of the blueberry mixture.

- Cut the butter into small squares and place them randomly on top of the cobbler.

- Sprinkle the ¼ cup sugar over the cobbler.

- Bake for 15 minutes. Turn down the heat to 350°F and bake for 35 minutes more or until golden brown on top.

- Let cool for 15 minutes before serving.

GROWING UP

-- -- -- -- -- -- -- -- -- -- -- --

Finding My Way . . . and My Voice

*I*t's amazing how some things really take you back in time. For me it's always been music and smell and taste—they conjure moments from my past and transport me back to when things seemed simpler, easier, and in some ways happier. It's about reclaiming your innocence, I think—letting a song reconnect you with the magical moments in your life.

I grew up listening to George Strait, Merle Haggard, Patsy Cline, Earl Thomas Conley, Dolly Parton, Charlie Daniels, Alabama, and Reba McEntire, among many others. Usually when there was a radio on in the Butler household or car it was tuned to a country station, but as a family we also developed a discerning ear for pop music.

My dad, especially, is a sucker for a great melody. At home, he wore out the Statler Brothers and Paul Simon, and on the road he teed up his groovy tape collection, which prominently featured the Captain & Tennille, Neil Diamond, Anne Murray, and Barry Manilow. He and I shared a deep love for the Carpenters, whose vocal and melodic triumphs still inspire me. Who sings with as much beauty and emotion and precision as Karen Carpenter? And to this day, when I hear "Forever in Blue Jeans" by Neil Diamond, I think of my dad and start to cry.

The motor home that took us on so many summer vacations was kind of a musical classroom. We would always have a tape playing, and we sang together so well that Dad briefly considered the possibility of us becoming a family singing group. I'm sure that it was on one of those long drives through the Midwest that I quietly began mapping out a plan to become a singer-songwriter myself.

When I was seven, I announced over dinner one night that I wanted to move to Nashville and be a country music singer like Dolly Parton. My mom was initially a little confused, but she smiled and said, "Okay, honey, you go for it."

Much later I realized she hadn't been humoring me. She and my father wanted their children to do whatever they dreamed of, however crazy it might sound. They didn't accept the notion that anything was out of reach for any of their kids, God bless 'em.

So, with their support, music began assuming a larger role in my life. I began to hone my chops in our small-town Church of Christ services in Quartz Hill, singing three days a week or whenever the doors were open. The preacher's wife was an excellent tutor, steering me through four-part harmonies and complex vocal parts and teaching me about projection and presentation.

Mr. Krauss, one of my elementary school teachers, was an opera singer. One day I overheard him telling my mom that I had a unique voice and ability. He signed me up to sing in public for the first time at the school Christmas pageant that winter. The night of the show I wore a little red velvet dress with white satin sleeves, and I can still remember nervously making my way through the side door of the auditorium. Everything was dark and the bleachers were full, my first packed house. My head was spinning, and I heard someone's voice echo through the hall. The spotlight hit me and I sang "What Child Is This," and when the applause rose at the end, I was hooked. I knew this was where I belonged.

A few months later, in the spring, I performed "Wouldn't It Be Loverly" from *My Fair Lady* in our annual talent show with my friend Carrie. Helen Barnett, a family friend, played the piano. She rehearsed with us at her house a couple times a week. My mom made us cute little hobo costumes, and on the night of the show Carrie and I gave it our all.

The next week Mr. Krauss asked me to lead the class performance of "The Impossible Dream" from *Man of La Mancha*. But I got a little confused, and instead of leading the group I turned and sang out to the crowd. The next day everyone on the bus made fun of me, asking, "Why did you not turn to the kids instead of the crowd? How stupid." My first real taste of rejection.

I was absorbed by anything having to do with music. I listened to Broadway musicals; gobbled up rock, pop, and country music; and studied the careers of great singers like Barbra Streisand, Frank Sinatra, and Elvis Presley. I loved it all—music transported me to a special place that was all my own, a little world where I could step onstage and create something beautiful all by myself.

Even though we were just a bunch of desert-rat kids without much money, my mom kept the cultural experiences coming. If *Madama Butterfly* was playing within driving distance, we'd go see it. We saw *The King and I* and *Les Misérables*, which I remember my mom had to save up for. And at the palatial Pantages Theatre on Sunset Boulevard in Hollywood, I was bowled over by the original *Phantom of the Opera* with Michael Crawford. It was the biggest, most lyrical and breathtaking thing I'd ever seen, as close to Broadway as you could get outside of New York City. And every year when it came on TV, I'd curl up to watch *The Sound of Music*—Julie Andrews was epic, mind-bending, one of my all-time favorites.

Exposure to these varied influences helped me find my own style. I knew I didn't really have a "traditional" country voice, but seeing so many different performers and listening to so many different kinds of music taught me an awful lot about how to perform diverse material, how to reach an audience, and what worked and what didn't.

I could feel myself getting ready for the next step.

– – – – –

Helen Barnett, who encouraged and supported my musical interests when I was a young girl, was the first real business-woman I ever met. Most women didn't own their own companies at the time, but Helen and her husband ran their construction company together as partners. She was brilliant, and I don't think I've ever met a smarter woman. Helen always encouraged my instincts and didn't see why I shouldn't pursue music. And Helen was somebody you just listened to.

When I was about twelve, I began taking piano lessons, and Helen started lining up local gigs for us. She would play the piano and I would sing. We played churches, weddings, showers, schools, and other events. We'd work most Saturdays and I'd make fifty bucks, which was great for a kid. I sang at more than a hundred weddings, and we'd do all the favorites of the era—"Wind Beneath My Wings" and so on. I may actually now hold the world record for most performances of "You Light Up My Life," after Debby Boone herself.

Then I got a part as one of the daughters in *The Pirates of Penzance* at the grand Lancaster Performing Arts Center, and Helen helped me get ready for that, too.

When I was older, Helen also helped me become a young businesswoman. She gave me pointers as I pulled my first company together, counseling patience and diligence, and she urged me to work hard and sacrifice. She always had confidence that my dreams could come true. I love her. Helen is one of the small handful of people who made a real difference in my life at a moment when it really counted.

– – – – –

I didn't enjoy school very much; it seemed like my mind was always elsewhere. I lay on the grass in our front yard and wrote songs and poems and spent a lot of time dreaming about being somewhere else, imagining what my life might look like one day.

In kindergarten we made our parents little commemorative plaques that were decorated with flowers made out of salted dough. My teacher, Mrs. Russell, watched carefully as everyone fashioned a white center in the middle of his or her flowers. I wanted to put a yellow center in mine, but she stopped me cold.

"No one puts a yellow center," she explained. "We only put white."

This made no sense to me. "Why? We have yellow paint," I asked reasonably. "Why do I have to put white in my flower? Why can't I have yellow?"

This threw Mrs. Russell for a bit of a loop. "Well, no one's ever done that before."

The other kids jumped in, pushing for the status quo.

"A yellow center? Why can't you make a white one like everybody else?"

I shook my head. "I'm putting a yellow center in my flower, thank you very much."

Mrs. Russell was not happy, but the experience was instructive. Not only did it open me up to how society will often try to make you conform to an arbitrary rule, it sometimes goes so far as to stifle your natural abilities and talents. Even though I was only five years old, something about this seemed important to me. In truth, I was a bit of an oddball in school, always creative, with my head in the clouds. I wasn't popular. I was headstrong, and people didn't always know what to do with that. (By the way, I kept that salted dough plaque; it hangs on my office wall today, crumbling a little bit every year, but it's still a powerful reminder not to let people put me in a box. And every once in a while when my daughter, Kendel Skye, has a tough day at school or out on the playground, I use it to remind her that she can have a yellow center, too.) *Think outside your box, KS.*

I didn't have stylish clothes, which didn't help. My mom

made most of what I wore, but she had her hands full trying to keep our family on track. She taught me that what you looked like was less important than who you were inside; clothes were not as important as character.

There was a crowd of Quartz Hill kids who were bullies, hard-assed "desert rats" who ran in a pack and often picked on weaker kids. They made fun of those who were less fortunate, and they were mean to me mostly because I was so stubborn and opinionated. When we were in the fourth grade, they decided I was a fat, ugly slob, and a steady stream of verbal abuse began.

One of the punks was a cement-headed kid named Bobby, who specialized in administering titty twisters to my budding breasts every time he caught me alone in the hallway. After one particularly painful run-in with Bobby, I vowed to get back at him. After the last bell that day, we all headed down to the pickup area where our parents would collect us. Bobby followed me all the way, shouting all the filthy variations on my name he'd cleverly come up with: Gina Butthole, Gina Buttlicker, Gina Buttface, and so on. I let him prattle on until we were at the curb, in front of dozens of kids and several carloads of parents. Then I calmly set my backpack down, turned on him before he could react, and punched him right in the face with everything I had. He went down like a sack of potatoes, and you could have heard a pin drop. Nose bleeding, he assumed the classic "vanquished bully" pose.

He blubbered, "She hit me!"

I knelt down close to him so no one else could hear and whispered, "That's the last time you're ever gonna touch me. And if you ever say another word to me, we're gonna do this again. We'll do it as many times as we have to until you get it through that little pea brain of yours that you're not going to bug me or any of the other girls anymore. Do we understand each other?"

He nodded, tears rolling down his cheeks, and just for a second I felt sorry for him. But I stopped myself before I actually apologized. And Bobby never bothered anyone again.

But it was a tough crowd, and the needling never really went away. Some years later, in high school, my junior class went on a college visit to UCLA, where some goons locked me in a Porta Potty and rolled it over on its side. They thought it was a pretty clever prank, until I came out crying and wet and smelling of waste. To this day, I can't go near a Porta Potty—it's like my own little "No wire hangers!" moment.

It drove me nuts to see people being picked on. I found myself drawn to—and sticking up for—some of my less fortunate classmates, which further distanced me from the cool crowd. There were a couple of special needs kids who caught daily grief from the class Neanderthals, and I wound up being their protector, standing up for them when the bullies tormented them and left them crying in a corner. Today, decades later, I become enraged when I see this type of abuse going on. I try to remember that because God loves the underdog, we all should; because He is a fighter for the weak, we should all fight for them; because He believes in us, we should believe in Him. These days I find myself watching with admiration as so many women around the world stand up to cruelty and bullying. In my heart I want everyone who's been picked on to just deck the guys who make their lives miserable, as I did with poor, stupid

Bobby. I know that's not always possible, but I pray fervently for all women who are stuck in abusive situations. When I was twelve and in the throes of adolescent hell, I wrote a poem that had a line I still think of from time to time: "I wish I had a thousand balloons so I could fly away from yesterday."

If only it could be that easy.

- - - - -

Wonder Woman was a big deal in the late 1970s and early 1980s. I loved her so much that my mom made me an outfit complete with a cape and gold rope. I identified intensely with her "girl power" message and thought that maybe I, too, could take control of my world the way she did. The more I tried out new things, the more I started to feel like Wonder Woman.

I didn't wear the costume just for Halloween—I wore it almost every day for a long time, and when I finally grew out of it, my mom put it in a shadow box for me. It hangs on my office wall today—next to the salted dough plaque—to remind me of where I came from. I always think, "If there was a fire, what would I take?" Number one would be my daughter, number two would be my pets, and number three would be my Wonder Woman shadow box. That's how much the idea of Wonder Woman means to me—she's a reminder that we are all full of possibilities, that we all have hidden strengths and courage we can use to better our lives and the lives of those we love. In my mind, my alter ego will always be Wonder Woman, a righteous protector, defender, and inspiration who overcame incredible obstacles to reach her fullest potential.

But deep down, of course, I still wanted to fit in. What

kid doesn't? In sixth and seventh grade I rather unexpectedly became a cheerleader, which briefly bought me admission to the in crowd. It was pretty great being "famous" at the middle-school level, being part of a team, sitting at the cool lunch table, and having friends on call every day. Some members of the cheerleader circle were a little snobby, but others became life-long friends. And even though I knew that being a cheerleader could be superficial and impermanent, it was a new experience, and I was nothing if not open to new experiences. My time shaking pom-poms in saddle shoes was fun, until I gained a few pounds and failed to make the team the next year. I was sad about it but not heartbroken; there was an air of inevitability to my being disinvited, I figured. So I turned my attention to other things.

My mom got me into softball. Ugh! I hated it. The girls on the team were pretty tough, and they didn't care for me at all. Sharply hit ground balls and my face did not make for a good combination, but I tried hard for my mother's sake. Only after I fell off a curb playing with my next-door neighbor and broke my arm did my mom finally let me quit.

While I was in my cast I signed up for another talent show. Even though I took my song selection very seriously, in retro-spect, singing Journey's "Open Arms" *with a broken arm* was probably ill-advised. The kids wasted no time laughing me off the stage, and for the next week they tormented me, holding their arms in makeshift slings as they sang "Open Arms" in the hallways. I was humiliated, but I had brought it on myself, I suppose. Just another step in the development of my soon-to-be very tough skin.

Then there was the reality of my love life, or rather the lack thereof. I didn't have a boyfriend like so many other girls did. In fact, when it was time for the senior prom, I had to ask one of my buddies to be my date. Eric was a die-hard rodeo rider, and we'd been close, platonic friends for a while. He was a loner, too, kind of in the same boat I was, so we decided to go to the prom together. He agreed to meet me at the dance after he rode in an event at Tehachapi that same afternoon. I was elated.

But on the night of the prom he was a no-show. I wandered around the dance alone. Then, as the lights went down for the last dance of the evening—when I was most dreading sitting by myself on the sidelines—the door opened and in came my Prince Charming. But he was on crutches and his left leg was in a cast—he'd broken his leg during his ride in Tehachapi. But, bound and determined to go to the prom, he hustled his way through the emergency room and just made it. We shared that one, beautiful dance while everybody whispered about how my cowboy wouldn't even let a broken limb keep him from being by my side that night. I sure wish all my challenges worked out like that!

– – – – –

I started thinking about making a little pocket money and exploring the "art of hospitality." I loved cooking and I really loved feeding everyone—the culinary and homemaking traditions that had been handed down from my ancestors were beginning to blossom in me, and I was starting to realize that taking care of people was much more satisfying than just making the cheerleading squad again. So I started poking around in the kitchen, and my mom was happy to have me as a pupil. Together we began exploring some of our family's culinary history.

Meanwhile, I did gymnastics on our front lawn, read poetry, and spent hours lying in the grass just thinking. One month I read *Leaves of Gold: An Anthology of Prayers, Memorable Phrases, Inspirational Verse and Prose,* which knocked me out. I loved Kahlil Gibran's line about inspiration: "Successful people are just ordinary people with extraordinary determination." I also cracked open the Bible, where I found one gem after another. One of my favorite passages is Proverbs 21:21: "He who pursues righteousness and love finds life, prosperity, and honor." When I was thirteen I tacked this up on my wall, and it became one of my guiding principles.

I didn't realize I was on my way to becoming an ambitious and driven person. I knew I needed to open my mind and heart to get ahead in a complicated and unforgiving world. I started getting myself organized. I made lists and goals and New Year's resolutions that were crossed off as I met each one. (I still do it every year.) I'd actually built up a little experience as a budding businesswoman. My first "official" job was selling lemonade in front of our house, and my second was picking vegetables, putting them in a wagon, and selling them to our neighbors. And growing up around a wildly improvisational and entrepreneurial father had inspired me.

I tried to build a Princess House business selling crystal items, such as candlesticks, vases, and cake domes, from door to door. Princess House kind of followed the Mary Kay home-sales model, and though the managers in our area initially thought I was too young, I made my bones at a sales meeting by showing the boss lady a new way to showcase products. They put me to work and I did pretty well for several months, but my mom had to drive me everywhere and that got old fast. It was just too hard to do without a driver's license.

But I wasn't about to let my transportation issues derail me from painting a bigger picture. I knew that whatever I wound up doing would spring from persistence and a willingness to work hard. I routinely prayed: "Dear Lord, no matter how hard times seem, no matter how bad I feel, I will try, try, try again. I will never admit defeat. I will persist."

I realized I thrived on challenge and uncertainty, and even drew strength from growing pains that had come with school, adolescence, relationships, and family. In my adolescent mind sometimes it seemed like I was a nail in a world full of hammers. But I was actually a reasonably well-adjusted kid growing up in a middle-class home with a hardworking family, living out a small-bore version of the American Dream. True, below the surface there were routine contradictions and conflicts; I was a thorny presence at home and school, and though my parents wanted the best for me, they didn't always know the right way to help me find it. But they sure tried.

— — — —

When people ask where I went to college I usually cite my many years attending the School of Hard Knocks. But that's just a snarky way of saying I was pretty much self-taught at every major juncture of my life. Which is not to say I had innate business ability, or a blinding insight into economics, or a handle on even the basic theories of how to run a small business. What I had was common sense and a thirst to succeed. I could see myself building *something* of value; I just wasn't sure what it would be.

When I was fifteen I decided to start my first real business. I needed a job, I needed some money—but I didn't want to work for anyone else. I didn't want to work at the Gap or McDonald's. I wanted to chart my own course and succeed or fail based on my own wits and energies and vision. I didn't have a lot of resources, not even a car. But I had seen my dad start so many businesses, master so many jobs, dive into so many new adventures. He won some, he lost some. But he never stopped trying. His experiences helped me determine that I would build something of my own. But what could I build?

I spent some long days mulling this over. Something in the food industry? No, too many permits, too much equipment. Some kind of laundry service? No, I couldn't afford to rent a space. My business would have to be mobile, something I could take home with me at the end of the day. It finally hit me: I was good at cleaning the house. I'd been doing it since I was a little girl. And how many times had I heard my mother and her friends lament the lack of affordable maid service? I could do that, I thought. I could open a cleaning service.

What would I need? Soap? A mop? A bucket? A broom? Some elbow grease? Everything I'd need would be cheap and readily available. And I was willing to do that which most people hated doing—mopping, scrubbing, and sweeping everything from furniture and floors to showers and toilets. I decided I'd be the best cleaner these people had ever seen.

There was another perk: It would help me ditch school. I could go clean houses and bypass a good deal of the boring classwork. So from that point forward I put in only enough time to get my diploma. I wasn't worried about getting into Harvard or USC or Berkeley—though despite the success I enjoyed later, believe me, there isn't a day that goes by when I don't wish I'd listened harder in school.

I told my friends and family what I had planned. My old Quartz Hill supporter Helen Barnett was especially excited. She said, "Well, if you're going to start a business, I'm going to help you with it. You need to create a profile, make a business card, compile references, and put a booklet together so that when you bid for jobs you'll have something that'll help them take you seriously."

She helped me design a blue folder and a little card that read, "Gina's Cleaning Company: If clean's your desire, we're for hire."

I set my sights on landing a couple of commercial clients to start with because I knew how picky housewives could be. There was an assisted-living place a mile from my house called Mayflower Gardens. One day I marched in, knocked on the manager's door, and gave him my little card and my little folder. I offered him a great price, 110% effort, a flexible schedule, and a money-back guarantee if he wasn't satisfied. I wouldn't take no for an answer, so he hired me. That's how I got my first real business started.

I knocked on lots of doors looking for clients, and having Mayflower Gardens "under contract" made it easier to line up more. Soon I was cleaning four businesses after school and on the weekends. Some of my friends started saying, "Oh, my mom wants to hire you," so I started cleaning people's houses.

Fifty-five bucks a house, which was pretty good money for a kid in 1985. Talk about long hours! I literally worked so hard my body ached at night.

Then my business exploded. The real estate boom hit the Los Angeles area, and the High Desert became a bedroom community with a lot of new people whose new houses needed cleaning! I started ditching school so I could take on more clients and make even more money.

I also spotted an opportunity in the commercial construction cleanup business. After a contractor finished building out an industrial space, there was a ton of junk and debris that had to be hauled off, and the space had to be cleaned up for the new tenants. So at the ripe old age of seventeen, I started bidding on final cleanup gigs at huge construction sites. Contractors wanted to (a) get me cheap, because they didn't think I knew what I was doing, and (b) amuse themselves by sexually harassing me, because not many seventeen-year-old girls visited their job site trailers. I gritted my teeth, sidestepped their advances, and made my pitch. And soon I was cleaning up big construction sites, digging the grout out, scouring dirt from the windows, removing stains and paint and gunk. It was backbreaking work on the cheap, a whole office or house for $250 or so. But even after I found out I was working for way below market value, I kept it up because it was steady money. Some contractors signed me up for multiple contracts.

Then I landed Blockbuster Video and International House of Pancakes, big clients that really buffed up my résumé. I seemed to spend an inordinate amount of time high up on ladders cleaning lighting fixtures and vents in these places, so this kind of work drove my price up to about $500. But the managers were still laughing behind my back; I was *still* significantly undercharging.

I got a government contract when the county broke ground on a new wing at Lancaster High School. I learned a lot about paperwork and codes and negotiating. I had to chase them for months to get paid, and I had to haggle constantly with the county officials.

All these experiences furthered my School of Hard Knocks education. Negotiations, proper bidding, ignoring intimidation and sexual harassment, sticking up for myself and my workers . . . all important items on the syllabus. And I was getting jobs, banking money, and building my business—pretty heady stuff for a determined teenager.

Lessons for Life and Business

Believe in yourself, walk with integrity, work hard, and trust in God.

MAMA'S FEEL BETTER SOUP

*S*ometimes life throws us curve balls, and comfort food can help an awful lot.

When we were growing up, every time my brothers or I got sick my mom would make this soup and we would feel better in no time. There is something about chicken soup that has a real healing element to it. My mom is a master at soups. She can whip up a soup so quick, so delicious, with everything in it but the kitchen sink, and it will always be amazing.

INGREDIENTS

10 cups low-sodium chicken broth

1 teaspoon garlic salt

1 teaspoon poultry seasoning

1 teaspoon cayenne pepper

3 large celery stalks, coarsely chopped

4 large carrots, coarsely chopped

Salt and black pepper

2 tablespoons vegetable oil

1 large onion, finely chopped

1 pound chicken breast, cut into small pieces

1 cup alphabet noodles

- Pour the broth in a large pot and stir on low to medium heat.

- Add the garlic salt, poultry seasoning, cayenne pepper, celery, carrots, and salt and black pepper to taste. Bring to a boil, then reduce heat and simmer.

- In a separate pan, heat the oil and sauté the onion and chicken until the chicken is almost cooked through.

- Add the onion and chicken to the broth and stir.

- When the celery and carrots are tender, after simmering for about 30 minutes, add the noodles.

- Cook until the noodles are tender.

- Season to taste and serve!

BANDLEADER

- - - - - - - - - - - - - - - -

Gigi Takes the Wheel

*W*hile I was building Gigi's Cleaning Company, I muddled through Quartz Hill High School. A pattern developed: I'd show up to class, do the minimum required, and then hustle off to work. School just didn't do it for me. By the time I was a sophomore in high school I was thinking, "Why do I have to sit here for hours?" I didn't understand. I could pass tests and fill out forms and write papers, but it didn't seem to be adding up to much.

The only class I really enjoyed was choral studies, because I loved music. I started singing solos and entered every talent show in the area. I was gravitating more and more to country music, following the instincts I'd had as a young girl on all those long family car trips when Reba and Dolly and Tammy had inspired me. When I was in high school, country music hadn't yet exploded as it would a few short years later, so among my friends country wasn't cool. But I wanted to be a country singer.

At the hair salon my dad had opened in a burst of entrepreneurial fervor, I met Shawnea Dwyer and started babysitting her two-year-old, Candice. Shawnea and her husband, Kevin, were a young Mormon couple in their early twenties, very godly, calm, and hardworking. I also started cleaning their house and ironing for them, and we spent a lot of time together. They could tell I wasn't fitting in at school and began encouraging me in countless little ways, reminding me that things would get better and that I would find my way eventually. Even though Shawnea was seven years older, we became close—she was like the big sister I never had. They took me on trips with them and gave me good, solid moral advice. They were wonderful Christian people.

One day Kevin handed me a book. "You need to read this."

It was a self-help book. I wrinkled up my nose and said, "My dad says this stuff is bull."

"Well, I won't say don't listen to your dad. But you might like it."

"Make up your own mind," Shawnea said. "You can do anything you want."

Shawnea and Kevin encouraged me to think for myself, believe in myself, and remember that I could achieve anything if I worked hard enough. In a way it was an extension of my parents' basic philosophy about their kids being capable of anything. But for a teenager without much self-confidence, it was good to hear it from someone other than my parents.

What a great influence the Dwyers were on my life. While I worked at their house I'd listen to their motivational tapes, and we'd talk about what it all meant. My favorite speaker was Denis Waitley. I eventually read all of his books and listened to all of his tapes. Soon I added Zig Ziglar, Joyce Meyer, and Max Lucado to the rotation. I'd fill my mind with positive thoughts and reminders: "I can do this, I can do this."

When I was sixteen I started cleaning for Joe and Judy, another young couple who were musicians. Joe was a bass player and Judy played guitar. They played most Fridays and Saturdays at a local dive called the Calico Saloon. When they found out how serious I was about singing, they invited me to join them one night. Since I was underage, they had to sneak me in the back door so I could join their set and sing a few songs.

They had a band, which was exciting. Joe would step up to the mic and say, "Now, our special guest Gina Butler is going to sing a couple songs for you, so make her feel welcome." I was terrified, but after a few appearances I started learning the ropes . . . and I was hooked.

– – – – –

When it came to music, I wanted to learn more. I started formally taking lessons. Vernon Bradley was a family friend who gave me my first official vocal training. He was a singer, and his love for music was so inspiring. And my dad's friend, retired fireman and weekend disc jockey Lee Rhodes, became one of my biggest fans. Lee seemed to know everything there was to know about country music, and I soaked it all up. I also started taking formal music reading and theory lessons.

My family went to church in Lancaster, where I met Roy Rogers's daughter. Through her I met Roy and his wonderful wife, Dale Evans, who lived in nearby Pearblossom. They were sweet and encouraging and took the time to offer some valuable guidance. Their advice was simple: Study with the best people I could find, and sing wherever and whenever I could.

I found a guy in Los Angeles named Robert Edwards who was a real pro. I drove down from the desert to Van Nuys every Tuesday for voice lessons with him. I practiced every day, running vocal drills and doing scales and stretching my voice this way and that. Robert taught me to discipline my voice, which he called "The Muscle," and he gave me real-world tips that I could apply right away—for instance, alcohol will strip the vocal cords and cheese thickens the tissues in the throat, so don't eat cheese or drink alcohol for three days before you're going to sing. This kind of information helped me focus. I wanted to be in perfect condition when I sang a four-hour gig, which in vocal terms was like running a marathon.

- - - - -

I was doing pretty well with my cleaning business, but the commute from the desert to L.A. for vocal lessons got expensive. So each trip, I tacked on a job cleaning for my great-aunt Susie, who lived in the San Fernando Valley in Encino Hills. I would clean her house first, then go to my vocal lesson. She lived in a huge villa down the street from Michael Jackson's place. Amazing view. She was a refined older woman and had always been very generous to my dad, serving as a second mother to him, and he adored her. The whole trip—driving down, cleaning Susie's house, squeezing in a lesson with Robert, and driving home—took several hours. Susie would pay me $65 to clean her huge house, and a one-hour vocal lesson cost $75. Including gas money I was in the red about $20 every week, but I thought, "I'm investing in my voice; I'm investing in myself." It paid for itself—the lessons were invaluable.

After a while, I felt ready to try something more ambitious as a performer. I started to network. I was halfway between Bakersfield and Burbank, two towns where bands and players and clubs were proliferating. It was a good time to be a country singer in Southern California.

I met a wonderful guy named Erik Halbig, an accomplished guitarist who was saving money and preparing to move to Nashville, where he'd eventually write some hit songs and produce a bunch of records. He agreed to help me put a band together. We enlisted a couple of solid players: Matt Henninger, a high school buddy, and Tim Troyer, a drummer who'd played all over the area. We dubbed ourselves Gina Butler and the Wild Silver Band and started rehearsing.

We landed a gig at Mayflower Gardens, the old folks' home that was my first and oldest cleaning client. The residents were a lively bunch, eager to have some live music to dance to, so the manager hired us and paid us $200 to play a two-hour set every Friday night. We split the money four ways and gradually refined the sound of the band.

I can't tell you how many times I sang "Grandpa (Tell Me 'Bout the Good Old Days)" by the Judds—probably more than they did. Although we played mostly "female" country songs, we covered Garth Brooks, George Strait, Desert Rose Band, Keith Whitley, Dwight Yoakam, and Buck Owens, too.

Some of the guys in the band thought it was weird for a girl to sing songs that had been recorded by guys. This threw me for a bit of a loop. Why couldn't I sing "Don't Close Your Eyes"? Or songs by Randy Travis or the Oak Ridge Boys or Ray Price? Why couldn't we do "I Can't Stop Loving You"?

"Well," they said, "it's just not done. You can't get your audience all mixed up."

But I wasn't having it. I knew that if a man could sing a song, a woman could sing it, too. I understood that a lyric might take on added or even unintended meaning, but I thought that could be interesting. The guys went along with it, but they thought I was being kind of pushy. Some years later when Lyle Lovett recorded "Stand by Your Man," the great Tammy Wynette anthem, I rejoiced; the thrust of the song shifted, and its resonance was deepened simply because a guy was singing it.

We got pretty good and started to line up some other regular gigs in the area. I put together a little portfolio with a band picture and a demo tape and knocked on lots of doors. Soon we were booked at VFW and Moose halls, old folks' homes, fairs and theaters, and clubs all over Canyon Country and down into Los Angeles. We'd go anywhere they would let us play.

After I finally graduated from high school, this became my life—cleaning houses and offices during the day, singing at night, making demo tapes every now and then, building a list of contacts, and quietly laying plans to eventually make a move to Music City, USA.

- - - - -

Playing clubs had its share of challenging moments. For instance, I've never smoked a cigarette voluntarily, but I played so many smoky bars that I worried about getting lung cancer. I hated the way I smelled after a four-hour gig. When I got home, getting the stench out of my hair and clothes was a chore; no amount of bathing and scrubbing seemed to fully remove it. And I always felt hungover the next day—not because I drank, but because the smoke congested me so completely that it felt more like a cold. To this day, I can't stand being in a smoky bar.

The School of Hard Knocks education continued onstage. I found that, even in a weird or hostile environment, I had a better-than-even shot at winning over an ornery audience, club manager, bouncer, or patron. Many of the joints we played served working-class, dancing-and-drinking Friday-night crowds, rowdy characters who could be hard to please.

It's kind of fun being the only sober person in a honky-tonk full of people determined to party. I loved watching everything unfold from the stage—people fighting, pairing up for the night, reuniting, breaking up, starting over, settling feuds, you name it. I learned so much from people's body language. Eventually I developed a pretty good ability to read people when I first met them, a skill that's come in handy many times since.

One weekend I booked a gig on the rough side of town in a country bar I hadn't been to before. It wasn't until we rolled up to play that we realized it was a biker bar. Pool tables, sawdust on the ground, fifty hogs lined up out front. Smoky, dark, mysterious. Lots of dangerous-looking guys in leather with beards and tattoos and piercings. You get the picture. Well, there I was in my white cowboy boots, fringed jean skirt, and a white fringed jacket with my hair all done up. I don't know who was more surprised—me or the bikers.

We set up while the patrons eyed us and whispered little jokes among themselves. The band members were looking at each other wondering, "Are we going to die?" I promised them everything would be okay—we were each going to take home $75 that night, so it was really a good opportunity. Assuming we didn't die, of course.

There were probably fifty or sixty people waiting for the show, drinking beer and eating peanuts and carrying on. There was a big guy wandering around the club, clearly the bikers' leader, and he was letting everyone know he was in charge. Six foot five, 350 pounds, boots, leather pants, swinging chain, the works. His sleeveless leather vest had "Kevin" stitched across the left breast.

Kevin started making fun of me before we even finished setting up the bandstand, laughing at me along with a handful of his buddies. "What are you doing here, little girl?" he started. "You don't belong here. You'd best take your cute little cowboy boots and get out while you can."

I ignored him and continued plugging in our gear, trying to smile over the fear that was growing. I thought maybe I could stay positive and not let him hurt my feelings.

Just then, almost on cue, my parents and some friends from church walked in and sat at an empty table right in front. I always told my mom where we were playing every weekend, and sometimes she and my dad would drop in and catch a set. As they settled in, I could see Dad's head swiveling around, taking in the sea of tough-looking bikers. And Mom pulled her purse close to her chest as if someone were about to snatch it away.

A few minutes later we kicked off the set with the Dolly Parton classic "9 to 5." I was singing with all my heart, trying to be brave. But as we finished all I heard was "You suck!" and "Go home, hillbillies!" Kevin's whole gang was laughing and chanting.

"We want Megadeth! We want AC/DC!"

"Take that little fringed skirt and get outta here!"

I tried to act like nothing was happening, but my parents were mortified—and my band was terrified.

My bass player looked at me and said, "We're gonna die!"

"No, we're fine," I said. "Why don't you try one? Maybe it'll be better."

So he gamely kicked off David Ball's "Thinkin' Problem."

Kevin smiled a little, but he still wasn't quite sold. At the end of the song there was no applause.

Next I belted out my version of Linda Ronstadt's remake of the Everly Brothers' gem, "When Will I Be Loved," always a great crowd-pleaser.

"You suck!" the bikers screamed.

"Go home!"

"Megadeth!"

I got so mad I finally stopped the band and yelled into the microphone, "Does it look like I should be singing Megadeth?"

Kevin was taken aback. He looked around a little sheepishly. "Not really, no," he mumbled.

I went for the jugular. "Then sit down, shut up, and let us play!"

Kevin approached the stage, now looking a little dangerous. You could have heard a pin drop. My parents were petrified, and I could tell my dad was about ready to step in. But I wasn't going to back down. This was it. The showdown. I thought for a brief second that all the band members might be soiling their pants.

I got all puffed up and yelled, "You want some of this?"

Kevin's eyes bored into me. Then he said, "You sure got a pair on you. Okay, little lady. Go ahead and sing."

He stuck out his hand and I took it. He jerked his head toward my parents. "Those are your folks?"

I nodded.

He stepped over and apologized to them. "Your daughter's got herself a fan for life."

Relieved, we went on with the show, and those bikers wound up being one of the best audiences we ever played to. And Kevin meant what he said. He began to come to all my gigs. Word got around and we started getting requests to play biker events. I started playing "biker night" at a local A&W root beer joint, and he would always pull up with a few of his crew. Then, incredibly, he started making me beaded scarves to wear onstage. And they were beautiful! Who knew a tough guy could be into crafts?

– – – – –

My parents were generally enthusiastic about my singing, but my mom really wanted me to go to college and have a life— get married, have kids, and so forth. Dad was worried, too. So despite my impatience to get out of the classroom and into the world, to please them I enrolled at Lancaster Community College.

During my first semester, the whole family went on vacation to Reno and my brother and I wound up poking around a video game convention at one of the casinos. We ran into a guy named Gary Puckett who was running a high-tech karaoke booth, and I got talked into singing a few songs. A small crowd gathered as I sang, and he was impressed. It turned out Gary was an L.A.-based songwriter/producer, and he offered to help me get a demo together.

That night I told my folks all about Gary's plan. They both knew I had been working hard to develop my skills and finance my dream of a career in music, so they decided to support me without putting up too much of a fight. They agreed to let me drop out and take my second semester tuition money to make a demo with Gary. I was thrilled. At the time it seemed like this demo would certainly be the answer to all my prayers, though it would prove to be just one of hundreds that I would make over the years.

Gary also joined me for the True Value Country Showdown, my first talent show competing for prize money. We sang "Islands in the Stream" by Dolly Parton and Kenny Rogers. We didn't win, but it was a great experience and I got a lot of positive feedback from the crowd.

A few months later, I met a guy named Don Norris, who played amazing classical guitar. We put a trio together separate from the Wild Silver Band and played a little gig every Friday night at the Bermuda Inn, which was basically a weight loss center for rich ladies. I'd get up and sing anything from Patsy Cline to the Everly Brothers. Even my skeptical friends and family members acknowledged that I was getting pretty good. Some local club owners even thought I might be the best singer in the area.

All this performing and bandleading experience was leading to one thing: Nashville. It was hard for me to tell if I was ready or not, but there was a growing sense of urgency about needing to jump off the cliff and try it—even if I flopped, I'd learn a lot from the experience. And gathering experience was what I was all about in those days.

My gut told me to approach Nashville carefully. So I decided to gather some intelligence and develop a sensible strategy. This turned into several fact-finding and networking trips over a year or so.

My first trip was a low-key affair. Mom and Grandma Edrie and I drove out in Edrie's Cadillac. I was going to meet Richard Bennett, a friend of Don Norris's who was producing Marty Stuart at the time. I brought him my demo, and he was very kind but thought I needed more work. I felt like I'd caught the scent. I'd sat down with a pro, and while he hadn't rolled out a red carpet, he hadn't laughed me out of his office, either. I took the experience as an inspiration to go home and work harder and get better.

A few months later I made a second trip to Nashville with my dad, this time to try out for Opryland USA. Unfortunately, it was a real bust. I didn't realize that live show performers at theme parks had to have vocal and stage training, dancing ability, movement, and so on. I could sing, but that was about it. I got onstage and sang two lines of "Here You Come Again," and a guy sitting out in the audience yelled, "Thank you! Next!" At least I'd tried. I think my dad was more frustrated than I was.

My third foray to Tennessee was a girls' trip with Sandy Stokes, a girlfriend from home. I spent a little time poking around the edges of the industry, researching the record companies, publishers, and management firms. I started to see myself living and working in Music City—but something was nagging at me, telling me that I wasn't quite ready to pull the trigger.

Four months later I flew back to appear on the TNN game show *10 Seconds*, a country-flavored *Name That Tune*. I didn't win, but I was on national TV. I made a demo of an old Sylvia song, "Tumbleweed," but I had a cold at the time and it sounded horrible.

On this trip I visited the Carter House in nearby Franklin, where the bloodiest battle of the Civil War had taken place. Raised mostly in California, I'd never realized how the Civil War had torn the nation apart. That day, touched by the stories of struggle and survival, I realized that in my heart I was a true Southerner. I've been a huge Civil War buff ever since.

When I got home I started singing in a Christian play that toured around L.A. and San Diego for several months, performing for youth groups and churches. Things were taking shape rather nicely, I thought. I was saving money, gathering more performance time, and learning about the world I wanted to join.

- - - - -

My first big break came performing at the Palomino Club in North Hollywood. The Palomino had been California's greatest country music club since 1949. Everybody had played there, from Roy Rogers, Johnny Cash, and Merle Haggard to Tammy

Wynette, Buck Owens, and Waylon Jennings. It was ground zero for both the L.A. scene and the "new country" movement that was taking shape. My set went well and I made a whole bunch of new contacts. When they invited me back, I took that as a sign I was headed in the right direction.

I decided to put a permanent band together. I'd been shuffling players and band lineups around for a couple of years, and I started to feel like some stability would help. I auditioned some local players and we practiced in my garage. I cashed in a life insurance policy and bought some new equipment and microphones.

Later that summer I went to see Garth Brooks for the first time, and watching him in full flight just confirmed everything I knew I wanted to do. But instead of moving to Nashville, an oddball opportunity popped up that I hadn't seen coming.

I had just turned twenty and had gotten a job singing at a campground out in Canyon Country. I noticed this tourist couple sitting and listening who seemed especially interested. After my set they came over and introduced themselves. They were country music promoters from Quebec, and they were looking for a singer to produce in Canada. They had some money and a big-time Canadian artist who was open to working with new talent. They asked me to come to Montreal, where they would find me a place to live and manage my career.

My parents met them and thought their plan sounded okay, that maybe it could be an adventure. But they wondered, if these guys were so good, what were they doing scouting for talent in a campground? But this was about the best offer I'd had, so I figured, Why not? Another chunk of on-the-job training would only help me in the long run.

So I closed down my cleaning business and moved to Montreal. It was a total culture shock. Everything was in French, and the locals didn't take too kindly to a little California girl. I felt isolated and lonely almost immediately. The promoters paired me with Dougie Trenier, a Canadian country guitar hero, and we started playing Thursdays through Sundays at a club called Le Legend.

We worked hard, playing gigs three or four nights a week and touring all over Ottawa and Toronto. Dougie was a great guitarist, and he had a tight band. He'd sing some songs and I'd do the harmony parts, then he'd say, "And now, here's little Gina Butler from California."

I found French Canadians to be pretty insular. They weren't particularly friendly to either Americans or non-French-speaking Canadians, so as a "little California girl" sharing the stage with a beloved Quebecois hero, I never really had a chance.

I lived with the promoters and paid them $200 a week for rent. What I earned onstage went to groceries, plus I cleaned their house and did their laundry. It wasn't exactly what I had envisioned, but I was too young and disoriented to put up much of a defense. I felt like this was becoming a Cinderella-type situation and very bizarre.

I'd call my mom and dad and say I didn't think this was right, but they'd just say, "Oh, you're fine, give it a chance."

But after six months in Montreal I was blunt with them. I wanted to come home. I quit Dougie's band, resigned from my Cinderella gig, and went home.

All my friends needled me: "We knew you'd be back!" That really bugged me. One of our family friends actually said I would never leave my mommy and daddy again.

But I wasn't listening. I was too busy putting together another band . . . and another plan.

— — — — — — — — — —

Lessons for Life and Business

Be strong and brave, and stick up for yourself, even if you get your butt kicked sometimes. No one will care more about making your dreams come true than you.

MOTHER LOVIN' MEATLOAF

*H*ere's a take on a classic dish that's all about comfort. Meatloaf is a nostalgic thing for many, and a healthy bite of nostalgia helps soothe the soul. When I close my eyes and catch a whiff of this recipe, I'm transported—to childhood, home, and family.

I've always loved meatloaf way more than I worried about the calories in it. But it's good to try to achieve balance, so in this recipe I've reduced the caloric content but kept that classic meatloaf flavor. Meatloaf can be really tasty when it's made with lower-fat ground beef or turkey.

INGREDIENTS

3 pounds lean ground beef or turkey

$1\frac{1}{2}$ cups Italian-style bread crumbs

$\frac{1}{2}$ cup Parmesan cheese, grated

1 large egg

1 cup milk

$\frac{1}{2}$ white onion, finely chopped

$\frac{1}{2}$ teaspoon dry mustard

$\frac{1}{2}$ teaspoon garlic salt

$\frac{1}{2}$ teaspoon dried rosemary leaves

$\frac{1}{2}$ teaspoon sage

$\frac{1}{2}$ cup plus 2 tablespoons ketchup

$\frac{1}{2}$ cup plus 2 tablespoons BBQ sauce

- Preheat the oven to 350°F.

- In a large bowl, mix all the ingredients together (except 2 tablespoons ketchup and 2 tablespoons BBQ sauce).

- Form the meatloaf into two oblong rolls and place in a 9 x 13-inch baking dish. Drizzle the remaining ketchup and BBQ sauce over the loaves.

- Bake for about 45 minutes, until brown inside.

DREAMCHASER

Building a New Life in Music City

*O*nce I'd flushed Canada out of my system and gotten resettled in Quartz Hill, I started up Gigi's Cleaning Company again, and within a couple months the second incarnation of Gina Butler and the Wild Silver Band was ready to take another musical step.

The lineup was solid. I brought old favorites Erik Halbig, Matt Henninger, and Tim Troyer back into the fold, and we added a couple of new guys, a bass player named Joe and rhythm guitarist Mike Broadway, who had a great name—and a prosthetic leg that he expertly hid beneath impeccably starched and pressed jeans.

Our first big gig was at a three-day Memorial Day celebration at the Riverside Casino in Laughlin, Nevada, about an hour outside of Las Vegas. As we pulled into the casino parking lot, full of excitement and nervous energy, I almost fainted. There it was, up on the massive marquee: GINA BUTLER AND THE WILD SILVER BAND. That was the first time I ever saw my name in lights.

That first night there was a guy in the crowd named Don Usherson, a Vegas-based entrepreneur who did a ton of bookings for the casinos and other venues around the Southwest. He approached me, said he liked my voice, and asked if we were looking for more work. Of course we were! So over the next few months we did some gigs for him in California and Nevada. I called him one night and asked if he'd consider booking us in Vegas, but he thought playing Vegas would be the worst thing for me. He then gave me the best advice of my life: "You're too young and sweet to be in Vegas. Careers end in Vegas, they don't start in Vegas. You need to go to Nashville."

All along I had felt it, too—ever since I was a little girl. And now a real pro had validated my instincts. Don was right. It was almost time to go to Nashville.

Onstage, musical lightning struck every now and then, and sometimes Mike and I were certain we could be the next big country duo. But there were some rough edges. Mike would occasionally show up half in the bag, and all I could do was pray that he'd get through the set without embarrassing us. Most nights we skated by, but one fateful night a record company guy came down to see us play, and Mike arrived thirty minutes late, seemingly inebriated. Right in the middle of "I Can't Help It (If I'm Still in Love with You)," he awkwardly climbed onstage, bumping into equipment and making a commotion. He plugged in his guitar and immediately started sawing away at a volume that was way too loud. There was an anxious stir in the crowd, and I wondered what the record company guy was going to make of all this. We had a lot at stake.

As Mike continued to "play," he got right up next to me and started jabbing me with the head of his guitar, playfully at first but then more insistently. It started to hurt, so I tried to twist away from him without making it look obvious. But he got in my face, daring me to do something. I'd finally had enough. I pushed him in the chest with both hands, not hard enough to hurt him, but with just enough force to back him off.

Unfortunately, he lost his balance, pitched backward off the three-foot-tall stage, and fell onto the dance floor with an "Ooof!" His artificial leg popped off and skittered across the floor, stopping right in front of the record exec. People screamed and pointed. From the stage I could see mortified faces everywhere in the room. The record executive shook his head sadly, dropped a twenty-dollar bill on the table, and left.

So much for our big break. We cut the set short and repaired to the small dressing area behind the stage, where I fired Mike on the spot.

I was learning that managing employees could be a real pain in the neck.

— — — —

Right around the time it became clear I needed to go to Nashville, I got involved with my first serious boyfriend. I was pretty sure I was in love, but I wasn't at all sure how that was going to play out.

Sam was a big handsome guy I'd loved from afar since I was a kid. He was older, and when I was nine and he was eighteen

I arrogantly assured my girlfriends that I was going to marry him one day.

One of them said, "He's fifty years older than you!"

Another said, "You can't marry him—he's all grown up."

But I didn't care, I was going to marry him. Sure enough, a decade later when I was twenty and he was twenty-nine, we started dating. Sam was truly my first love. He was Cherokee Indian and Irish, the most beautiful man I'd ever seen. He was six-two and looked a lot like George Strait—better, actually.

Sam was very supportive of my music career. In fact, he would go to many of my shows with me. One in particular stands out. For months I tried to get a gig at this club in LA. The owner was a woman who played hard to get and would never commit to giving us a shot. Some of the guys told me she was notorious about treating bands badly, but I love a good challenge, and I kept at it until I finally wore her down.

Sam rode with the band and me to the gig. The owner took one look at my fringed red skirt and started giving me a hard time about being a "hick." I asked her point-blank what her problem was, but she just scowled.

This place was a post—*Urban Cowboy* kind of joint where the bandstand was behind a curtain of chicken wire, in case anybody was moved to throw a bottle at the band. When we started playing, about five people in the back started heckling us and making fun of me in particular. Then they started throwing stuff at the chicken wire—beer bottles, salt shakers, French fries, you name it. Everybody started laughing and throwing things. I realized the owner was the ringleader! She'd started the ruckus with the five people in the back. So after the first set I went over to her.

I said, "Am I doing something wrong here?"

"No, you're fine."

"Why are you making fun of me?"

"Because you're easy to make fun of. What's the big deal? I paid you. I can do whatever I want."

"You're not supposed to be making fun of the band."

We started the next set and she started making fun of me again, cussing and throwing cups and bottles at me.

I finally had enough. From the stage I threw down my mic and I said, "You and me, outside, now."

She followed me out to the parking lot, where I got right up in her grill.

I said, "Why don't you make fun of me right now to my face?" Her eyes lit up and in that instant I realized that deep down she was hardened white trash—more than ready for a fight.

And we went at it, just duking it out. I got the best of her right away—the joys of youth!—but my boyfriend jumped in and tried to pull me off her.

Some of the bikers in the crowd joined the effort to separate us as one of my bandmates said, "Are you really doing this, fighting the bar owner?"

Eventually they pried us apart.

She panted, "You're fired!"

And I spat back, "No, I quit, And you're paying us or I'll drag you back out here and beat you down again."

She paid us and we took off, an early night for once. I never figured out what her deal was. She was just mean. I was starting to understand that the average club or bar owner belonged to a rather eccentric group. It wasn't my first run-in with a bar owner, and it wouldn't be my last.

Sam was established professionally in Southern California, and without being selfish about it he made it clear he wasn't interested in moving to Tennessee. But there was a little voice inside me reminding me that if I didn't try the music route in Nashville, I might look back one day and regret it.

I told Sam I loved him, but I had goals and I needed to pursue them. "Just give me six months," I said. "If I can't get anything going, I'll come back."

He just shrugged and gave me a little squeeze. I expected a bit more emotion from him at this point, but thought, well, he's older and wiser. He knows how to keep his cool.

One Saturday I went outside to talk to my dad, who was working on his car. I said, "Dad, I'm moving to Nashville. It's now or never. I've got to go. I'm doing it."

He studied me for a long moment, and then I could see acceptance in his eyes. Having gone for it so many times himself over the years, he recognized a chip off the old block.

I gave him a hug and ran inside to tell my mom. I had been to Nashville several times by this point, and there was honestly nothing about it that was intimidating to me. I knew she didn't want me moving all the way across the country, but we could both feel in our bones it was time for me to go.

- - - - -

In August 1994 I sold my cleaning business to one of the girls who worked for me. I paid off all my bills and had $500 in cash left over. No job, no friends, no place to live—but lots of faith in God. I was ready.

Courtney Palladini, a Lancaster kid who'd just graduated from high school, was a big fan who used to hear the band play. She came from a big family and wanted a change, so I invited her to move with me. She thought about it for about thirty seconds and then said, "I'm in." She packed up and was ready to roll before I was. I loved her energy.

My parents offered to help us move. They loaded up their truck with our stuff, Courtney and I climbed into my little white Pontiac, and off we went. Our two-vehicle convoy headed east, retracing many of the same steps we'd taken on our summer vacations. There was a lot of laughter and conversation as Arizona, New Mexico, Texas, and Oklahoma rolled by, and we reminisced about visits to grandparents, blueberry fields, bakeries, and fishing holes. I was excited as I thought of what lay ahead.

Through deserts and cities, across prairies and badlands, past farms and cemeteries and ranches and truck stops, I marveled at how big and bold and beautiful America looked. I was starting to understand it all from the perspective of a woman who was now about to "step out on faith" and try to find her place in the world—a woman who was willingly leaving everything she knew behind. Something told me I should have been scared. But I wasn't. I couldn't wait to get there.

Our first night in Nashville we stayed at the Hallmark Inn on Thompson Lane. I missed Sam terribly, and as soon as we checked in I called him.

"I'm here. And everything's going to be fine."

His voice was flat. "I can't believe you did this."

I squirmed a little. "I know. And I'm sorry, but it's hard enough to do this without you being mad at me. Just give me six months. Then I'll come back to Quartz Hill, and we'll get married and have a life together. But I have to try this."

He mumbled something forgettable and wished me luck, but his heart wasn't in it. Looking back, I think that might have been the moment when he officially shut me out. Although we enjoyed each other's company, there was a fatal flaw in our relationship. He was a desert rat at heart and had no use for the "city" adventures I craved, and he knew I would never be the kind of docile woman he was really looking for. Sam was ready to put down some roots, and I was headed in a completely different direction. We ultimately broke up.

I found myself wondering if I'd ever find true love. It's not written anywhere that love has to happen to everyone. Clearly, I hadn't met the right guy. I thought maybe I'd go to church one day and wind up sitting next to Mister Right. You never know. I was different and I knew it—I was quirky and would be a hard fit for almost everyone I met.

I was on a journey—a voyage of discovery, moving toward a fuller understanding of who I was meant to be. And I was nurturing a fervent hope that one day I might feel better about the woman I saw in the mirror.

– – – – –

Courtney and I found an apartment in West Nashville off Charlotte Pike. The neighborhood was kind of run-down and scary, but the price was right. My parents stayed a week and helped us get settled. We scrubbed everything down, set up house, hung pictures, bought beds, rented some furniture, and filled the fridge with groceries. The loneliest day came when my parents drove off and left us to our own devices.

I remember thinking, "How do I start my life?"

We needed to find work. I was worried, but without much fanfare, Courtney walked across the street and got a job at Walmart.

A friend back home had given me the phone number of a Nashville songwriter named Tom Bruner. Doing my best to be fearless, I cold-called Tom and asked if he'd be willing to meet and give me some advice. He invited me over to his home office in Brentwood and spent some time with me. He didn't think my demos were good enough to get me started and recommended that I keep refining my sound and my songwriting. Ordinarily, this could have been deeply disappointing to a young, ambitious performer, but I was thrilled to be getting focused advice from such an established industry figure. Tom was a good man, and he asked if there was anything else he could help with.

I dove right in. "Well, I need a job. Do you know anyone who might be hiring?"

He smiled. "My daughter works at Red Lobster. I think she said they were interviewing."

The Red Lobster restaurant was in Cool Springs, about twenty minutes from where I lived. Even though I'd never been a waitress before, I'd certainly picked up the lingo and knew my way around an eatery through helping my mom and dad in their various restaurant ventures when I was a kid. I thought, "How hard can it be?"

Tom loved my attitude and had his daughter put in a good word for me. He invited me to stay in touch, and—boom!—I had started building my Music City network.

Red Lobster hired me right off the bat and I started work the next day. Now, I'd never really been around many Southerners, and I learned right away I had to listen carefully, because when customers would order I often had trouble understanding them.

Friedshrimpfrenchfries started to make sense after a while, and navigating the various accents was intriguing; it was like a new language to me. There were thick, rich, honeyed tones and high, tight, brittle ones. There were people who talked super fast and people who spoke so slowly I thought I'd nod off listening to them. There were elegant, lilting, aristocratic sounds, and harsh, grating, barking rumbles. And all of it right there in the Red Lobster!

I also learned that most Red Lobster customers were devotees of the bargain—in other words, they could be kind of cheap when it came to leaving gratuities. It was fairly common to work your butt off and receive only a single dollar as a tip. We had to take orders, deliver drinks and appetizers, make the salads, serve the food, orbit around to make sure everybody at every table was happy, and then total up the checks, collect payment, and clean the table. We didn't even have busboys. You had to be organized to make each shift a success.

Although I would get annoyed whenever a table would stiff me on the tip, I went from being irritated to finally understanding that, for some of these folks, splurging for a meal out at Red

Lobster was a big deal financially. I worked on becoming a little more patient and humble.

I had cleaned houses, but I had never worked as part of a big staff before, so the politics and pettiness at Red Lobster were fascinating to me. My manager was very belittling and mean-spirited. She made the servers feel useless, and she actually harassed us a bit. I remember thinking, "I hope if I get into power I'll never treat people like that."

Now, I'm not saying I haven't had my own ups and downs learning how to treat others, and I haven't always been the nicest person in the world. But I truly do try to make the people in my life feel loved and special whenever I can.

One great thing about Red Lobster was that I could eat half-price salads and soups almost every day, and if something was cooked wrong and sent back to the kitchen, I always tried to snag it first. I never went hungry while I worked at the restaurant, which was great during those lean times. I could start my day with oatmeal and a potato, work my shift, and bring home leftover chicken. Whenever my mom would call and ask if I was eating properly, I could truthfully say yes, so she didn't have to worry too much about me.

My new job put me into contact with a bunch of interesting people from the music business. Cool Springs is in one of the wealthiest counties in America—because many of Nashville's business leaders and entertainment figures live there. And when I first moved to Nashville, there weren't many restaurants to choose from, so Red Lobster was a pretty popular spot for some of these folks.

Lots of songwriters, executives, performers, and businesspeople who lived in the Franklin area came in. I waited on Faith Hill, George Jones, Charlie Chase, Tanya Tucker, Tim McGraw, the Judds, and many more. And that first year rubbing elbows with them taught me a bunch of lessons about how to handle myself as I began to wind my way through the Music City maze.

George Jones and his wife, Nancy, were regulars. They always came in for *friedshrimpfrenchfries*. And we all fought to serve them because they always left a fifty-dollar tip! Contemporary Christian superstar Steven Curtis Chapman would bring his whole family in. "One for the Road" Ray Stevens was there once or twice a week. Back then we had a smoking section, where Jerry Reed would commandeer a booth and smoke a whole pack while he was having lunch—what a character. Tons of songwriters and producers and lawyers and record people ate there.

One day I got a major lesson in patience and grace. I was waiting tables and Naomi Judd and her husband, Larry Strickland, came in. She was wearing a fur coat and I was so nervous. As a rabid fan of the Judds, I'd followed their incredible journey for years. Tongue-tied, I took their order and was coming back out of the kitchen with their salads, bread, and sweet teas when I tripped. Half the contents of the tray wound up on Naomi's fur, mostly from the extra ramekins of Thousand Island dressing she'd ordered. The coat looked like it had just been salvaged from a Dumpster.

I could barely croak out a soft "S-s-s-sorry . . ."

But Naomi said, "Honey, it's just a fur coat, not a broken heart. But if you could get me a towel real quick that would be great."

I felt so bad. But because she was gracious and kind, the sting floated away. She didn't have to be like that. She could've gotten me fired. I'll never forget how she made me feel. I think about that exchange every time I start to lose my temper about something. People may forget the time or date when something happened, but they will never forget how you made them feel.

One night a fascinating songwriter named Kim Williams came in with his lovely wife, Phyllis. Kim wrote so many hits for artists like Joe Diffie, Garth Brooks, and Randy Travis that I can't count them all. He had been badly burned and disfigured in an accident, but his attitude about life couldn't have been sunnier. He'd come in twice a week and talk to me about what he was writing and working on. He invited me to his office to play him my demos, and we listened to all the songs in his catalog. He encouraged me to write more. It really impressed me that a man of his accomplishments would give me even an hour of his time.

One day, as the holidays were approaching, he asked if I had a place to go for Thanksgiving. When I shook my head, he smiled and said, "Come over to our house for dinner."

Kim introduced me to other writers. He was booked with his fellow platinum writers, but we joked about how one day I'd be in his league. He continued to help me meet people in the business and start getting writing sessions set. Every once in a while, he and his wife would invite me to social functions, or they'd drag me along when they went shopping. I'd usually wind up with a bag of groceries.

Kim would ask, "Do you need some chicken?"

I'd say, "No, no. I'm fine."

But he'd look at his wife and she'd cluck, "You're hungry, you need something."

And she'd load up a bag of apples or a big package of chicken. They were the sweetest people, so generous and caring. I was so sad when Kim died in 2016. It always hurts a little harder and deeper when such a good man is lost. I've remained in touch with his daughter Amanda, who's become a very gifted singer-songwriter in her own right.

– – – – –

My faith came in handy as I worked to build my new life in Nashville. In January 1994 a massive ice storm hit town. Traffic came to a standstill, roads were iced over, the airport was closed, people lost power, and pipes froze. Within days, the authorities were fearful that senior citizens and children and animals would fall prey to below-freezing temperatures.

I was at work at Red Lobster when the storm hit. Most people went home immediately, but I wanted to stay and make a little bit more money. When I finally clocked out, I realized I hadn't paid much attention to the weather forecasts. All I had to fend off the cold was a very lightweight jacket.

The parking lot looked like a scene from the Ice Age. My car's windshield was caked with three solid inches of ice. I tried to scrape it off, but that didn't work, so I banged on it with my jack handle, which cracked the glass. Finally, enough ice fell away that I could see well enough to get on the road.

A California desert rat, I had never really driven in heavy winter weather before, and ice was a whole new experience for me. As I crept out of the lot, I could see cars sliding off the roads. There were wrecks and pileups everywhere. I lived only about twenty minutes from Cool Springs, so I figured I could make it if I kept calm and stayed in the slow lane.

I was halfway home, just crossing the overpass onto the 440 freeway in a dense cloud of fog and swirling snow, when an eighteen-wheeler in front of me hit a patch of black ice, lost its traction, and began an inexorable slide toward the shoulder. In what seemed like slow motion, it jackknifed right off the road. Then I hit the black ice, skidded into a guardrail, and spun into a ditch.

I sat there, paralyzed. What was I going to do? Back then, I didn't have a cell phone. The road was impassable, so it was unlikely anyone else was going to come along anytime soon. More important, I had only my lightweight jacket, no scarf or gloves. I looked down with dismay and realized that I was still wearing my thin canvas tennis shoes from work.

I took a deep breath and got out of the car, steeling myself against the cold. I tried to dig out the snow and ice from around my tires with my bare hands, but within a minute or so I could feel my fingers freezing up, like a million needles jabbing me all at once. I was totally stuck in the ditch. I was so frightened. I crawled back into the car, fired up the heater, and started praying. If ever I needed the strength of God, it was now.

Finally, I worked up the nerve to try again. I got back out and made my way to the front bumper, which was stuck in a two-foot snowdrift. I found some firm footing and started pushing with everything I had. At first nothing happened. The needles came back, and my fingers started freezing again. I closed my eyes, counted to ten to calm myself, and started praying again.

And suddenly I stopped feeling cold. The pain in my fingers went away, and I could feel the car below me tremble, rock back and forth, and then finally roll back out of the drift. When I opened my eyes, the car was sitting on the shoulder, clear of all the ice and snow. Somehow I had pushed it back onto the road. It was a miracle.

I couldn't believe I had made it home. It was a reminder that any time I've been in a pickle, somehow God's always been there to deliver the extra oomph I needed to get through. It's almost as if He knows how hard it is to be a single woman making her way in the world. I believe He gives His daughters a little push when they need it the most.

- - - - -

Erik Halbig, my bandmate from California, used to play at a popular club in San Bernardino where a guy named Dave Byrd was a DJ. Dave was also a budding personal manager, and he introduced me to an interesting Canadian couple who'd been soaking up the burgeoning local music scene.

Hazel and Bryan Lyons owned a huge international trucking company based in Toronto called Harrow, and their business took them all over America. They loved music and had hatched a plan to sponsor a musical act as part of a promotional push. Garth Brooks was hot then, and country music dominated the charts, and the Lyons were eager to tap into the "new Nashville." Dave had convinced them to get involved on the ground floor with a "baby act"—someone like me.

So Hazel and Bryan came out to Nashville and we all just fell in love with one another. I signed a six-month contract with

Harrow on December 14, 1995, to perform under the banner "Harrow Presents" and to appear at a variety of corporate and promotional events. Hazel and Bryan began grooming me, buying me clothes and equipment. We'd hit the clubs and go to the Wildhorse Saloon and study other performers. They helped me with my confidence and stage presence.

One day they announced that they wanted to fund a demo and start shopping me to record companies. I was ready. I brought in Ken Harrell to produce a four-song demo. Ken was a wonderful guy, always proper and gentlemanly. He was an amazing songwriter, with several of his own hits. The demo came out beautifully and helped me take a shot at the big leagues. Several A&R executives, including Capitol Records' legendary Steve Stone, gave me a listen, and although no one was ready to sign me outright to a record deal, I was now on their radar.

I formed another band with Erik Halbig and my old high school buddy Tim Troyer, who was now living in Nashville. Tim was adorable, one of the only guys in my life who I believe truly loved me. He was kind and good, always willing to do anything for me. We had always been just friends, but this time around I could sense that his feelings for me had deepened. He soon made it plain that he was interested in more than just a job. He wanted a relationship. Unfortunately, I couldn't be bothered. I was blinded by ambition and working virtually around the clock cleaning houses, waitressing, and chasing my musical dreams. Who had time for romance? Although we dated awhile, I kept him at arm's length. Ultimately I would break his heart and lose him as a friend because I couldn't grasp how good he would have been for me. I know he would have married me, and we could have been happy. But my head was in the clouds, and my eyes were full of stars. I couldn't see him for who he was, and that is one of my everlasting regrets.

We got a job as a house band at a club called Tilly and Lucy's in Hermitage, a thriving suburb east of Nashville, where President Andrew Jackson's cotton plantation was located. The club was packed almost every night. Trace Adkins and his band had been the house band but had recently signed with Capitol Records, so I rented his equipment from him and took over the gig.

We played every Thursday, Friday, and Saturday night for almost a year. We got our chops down and became a pretty decent band. It was great training. A man named Tim Nichols came out one night. He was a songwriter who used to be in the group Turner Nichols, and he'd written a few hits, including "Live Like You Were Dying," "Cowboys and Angels," and "A Baby Changes Everything." We became friends, and I started singing some of his songs. He played me "Heads Carolina, Tails California," and I thought, "Man, that's gonna be a smash." I asked if he'd let me cut it, but he just smiled ruefully. It was already on hold with a young singer named Jo Dee Messina, who would rocket to fame with her amazing version of it.

That kicked off her incredible career.

- - - - -

Through Hazel and Bryan, I also became the spokesperson for the Western Star Truck Company's lost and missing children campaign. I went all over the country to trucking conventions speaking and singing, and I did a video and sang a song with

John Walsh from *America's Most Wanted*. Both Harrow Trucking and Mack Trucks were involved in promoting the events, and I learned a lot about trucking and transportation—and marketing.

Unfortunately, costs piled up and it became clear to Hazel and Bryan just how difficult it was to break a new act. Though we remained friends, after about a year the whole thing just sort of ended. I went back to cleaning, playing three nights a week, and writing new songs. One step forward, one step back—the story of my life!

One night a guy named Jim Wise came into Tilly and Lucy's. He was a singer-songwriter who had made a few records, including a mini-hit in 1997 called "She Wants to Drive My Truck." He took a shine to me and we became friends. He took me on the road with him to open a few of his shows and started helping me with career advice, so I asked Jim to manage me. He quickly assumed an outsize role in the life of the band, which not everyone was happy about. When Jim and I got involved romantically, my loyal and true buddy Tim Troyer had finally seen enough. He threw in the towel, went back to California completely heartbroken, and never spoke to me again.

Jim and I didn't last long, and before I knew what hit me I'd lost a drummer *and* a manager, and I was all on my own again.

- - - - -

After a couple years in Nashville, I finally had enough money to rent a decent place. I found a great little two-story condo down by the Cumberland River, right across the road from the picturesque Blue Moon café, which sat out on the water. I had two bedrooms and one and a half baths and felt like I was finally moving up.

About this time I started cooking a lot and having people over for dinner. I'd call my mom and go over different recipes with her, and it kept us together despite all the miles that separated us. I missed her, and I was glad we had this tie—culinary adventures were still part and parcel of the Butler family experience. Every time I cooked I thought of her and missed her. I read cookbooks and watched cooking shows and daydreamed about doing something in the kitchen that might one day land me on TV.

As Christmas rolled around, I quit working at Red Lobster and went home to visit my parents. For a brief moment I felt a pang of homesickness, and I almost thought about staying. Almost. But then I spent some time revisiting my old stomping grounds, which reminded me that I'd made the right decision moving to Nashville. Although I missed my folks and some of my friends, I realized I didn't miss Quartz Hill or its small-town mind-set. It all seemed so provincial to me that by the end of the holidays I couldn't wait to get back to Music City—to a new band and the brand-new Tennessee chapter of Gigi's Cleaning Company.

- - - - -

I'd been collecting cleaning clients via my Red Lobster customers and their friends on an informal, small-scale basis, so I decided to make it official and revive Gigi's Cleaning Company. I thought there was plenty of room in a metropolitan area like Nashville for one little company to thrive, especially since I knew I had a good formula and had worked out most of the bugs back in Quartz Hill.

I set about relaunching the business by the seat of my pants, applying the lessons I'd learned from building the first version of the company. I didn't have a lot of money to work with, so I kept it simple and stuck to basics. I handed out, pinned up, and slipped under windshield wipers a ton of flyers all around the neighborhoods of Franklin, Brentwood, Green Hills, and Belle Meade, where I thought I'd find affluent people willing to hire domestic help. I tried to distinguish my flyers from all the others by dropping them off at front doors with a little ribbon and visibly wedging them on the sides of mailboxes.

I gradually picked up some new clients, and most of them were pleased to find that I did an honest, thorough job at a fair price. Many recommended me to their friends, and the word of mouth was like a rush of oxygen to the new business. I'd get a call and someone would say, "Hey, I got your number from my friend Betsy at the country club, and she said you did a great job. Can you come over and give me a quote?"

Soon I had about three dozen clients. My schedule was staggered: I'd do two or three houses a day, five days a week. Then I'd do the rest the following week. When the band worked really late or had an out-of-town gig, I'd add a sixth day to that particular week and double up the houses. The clients were all understanding, mostly because I'd earned their trust—I worked hard for them and faithfully met their needs.

This was a different exercise than cleaning houses in the High Desert, where basic service and cleanliness met most folks' standards. Here, in some of the most affluent neighborhoods in America, I was learning how to meet higher standards and establishing a solid reputation for quality, value, discretion, and consistency. I found that I had a knack for it. I really enjoyed *exceeding* people's expectations. It gave me a glimpse into what it's like to do something better than the competition.

I liked the feeling—I liked it a lot.

- - - - -

Everything in life is about timing. And how you deliver and stage a musical performance is all about timing. When you're the only sober person in a room, you learn how to read people quickly. Knowing how to read someone's tone and body language is important. I may not have gone to business school, but what I learned negotiating with bar owners, babysitting musicians, and playing in hundreds of honky-tonks proved to be priceless.

If you want to be in the music industry, you can't be thin-skinned. On top of the amorality and overt larceny I witnessed, there's just too much rejection, negativity, and criticism for fragile people. You constantly hear, "Your song isn't good enough," and "Your voice isn't strong enough," and "You're not skinny/pretty/sexy enough." If that wasn't enough, in the post-Shania world there was a massive amount of pressure to show some skin, to bare your tummy. The pressure! It felt like a woman artist's approach had to be all about sex appeal.

But I was on a mission. I started writing songs again, really seriously writing. I kept up my vocal lessons and started looking for work at the clubs in downtown Nashville. We scored a gig as the house band at Tootsie's Orchid Lounge.

Tootsie's is one of the legendary Music City watering holes, where innumerable performers got their start. It was originally run by Tootsie Bess, an empathetic supporter of musicians who was known to loan money, food, and couch space to struggling singers and songwriters. Superstars like Roger Miller, Waylon Jennings, Terri Clark, Dolly Parton, Harlan Howard, Ray Price, Bobby Bare, and Kris Kristofferson were regulars. One story goes that Willie Nelson, then just another songwriter looking for a break, performed a new song in the bar one night, and Patsy Cline happened to be there. The song was "Crazy," and Patsy jumped all over it.

We performed every Tuesday and Friday from 6:00 to 10:00 at Tootsie's for a year and a half. The catch was that the house bands only worked for tips, which routinely made for some pretty slim pickings, as we played a majority of our sets for penny-pinching tourists. After a while, we started openly discussing the wisdom of continuing at Tootsie's, so the owners started giving us $35 per person. That was for a four-hour set with no breaks.

We moved down to Robert's Western World on Lower Broadway, which JesseLee Jones had just bought from its founder Robert Moore. Jesse was a great guy, one of us, a musician who had chased a few dreams himself. He played on the weekends at Robert's with his band, and most people didn't know he actually owned the bar. His band had that "traditional" country sound down, and could absolutely smoke rockabilly. With ringing, twangy guitars and a driving stand-up bass, they played a ton of classics, so when Jesse hired us to play Thursday nights, we fit right in because we played stuff from the '40s, '50s, and '60s. A little group of fans started showing up to see us every Thursday, and we settled in for a two-year run.

The main clubs downtown—Tootsie's, Rippy's, Legends, The Stage, Robert's—were always in a state of friendly but determined competition, and the rivalries were part of what made Music City so rich and interesting. I still hit the clubs once in a while, because they're all great places for people-watching. Now that I'm "retired" as a performer, I fondly recall the club scene as an important stop along my musical path.

Through this period the Wild Silver Band maintained basically the same lineup: Joe Weber on bass, Butch Simmons on drums, Bob Hatcher on guitar, and fiddler Heather Smith. We'd have a rotating series of guitar players, including "Shreddy" Kevin Mason, one of the nicest guys around, a great family man, and a heck of a player. Sometimes when we went on the road we'd add another player or two.

Joe Weber, whom I'd met at a writers' night at the Boardwalk Café, became my North Star, my constant collaborator. He was always there for me in a lot of ways, and he did his best to help me musically whenever he could. I did a demo with him, and we started writing together.

I found Jim Murphy, a songwriter who lived in Hendersonville, about twenty miles outside Nashville. Jim was legally blind, so I'd drive out every Wednesday and we'd write. We wrote a hundred songs together, but the only cut we ever got was when they used our song "Big City" on the TV series *Undercover Boss*. I love getting a tiny little check from BMI for that.

Meanwhile, the Wild Silver Band played everywhere. I became a grassroots hustler. I would call city and county and state fairs and send them our bios and a demo. A fair in one county would hire us, and then recommend us to other county fairs. Word of mouth, just like in the cleaning business.

We played the Boardwalk Café, Douglas Corner, 5 Spot,

Sage, Legends, you name it. I tried to get on the talent shows at the Wildhorse. Anything I could do, I'd scrounge around and find it, figure out a way to do it. We went to Alabama, Texas, Arkansas. We even went to Switzerland.

We were constantly adding to our repertoire, and eventually we had enough material down for four or five sets—several hundred songs plus all the originals we were writing on our own. Gina Butler and the Wild Silver Band could play pretty much anything, in any style, on any given day. It was an eclectic mix, moving easily between country and the kind of pop I'd grown up listening to.

– – – – –

While I was building up my cleaning business again, I landed what I thought would be a great gig for the Wild Silver Band at a bar in the area. We became the house band and were contracted to play every Thursday, Friday, and Saturday night.

They put our name on the marquee out front. GINA BUTLER AND THE WILD SILVER BAND, it read. But in short order the "G" and the "R" fell off, and nobody ever quite got around to fixing it. So during the entirety of our residency at the bar it read INA BUTLE AND THE WILD SILVER BAND.

My friends had fun with that one. "Can't wait to see Ina Butle—Ina Butle rocks!"

After a few weeks at the bar, I noticed that even when the crowds in the club were thin, there was always a bunch of people congregated at the motel-style bungalows out back, behind the club.

I saw that the same women always seemed to check into

the bungalows on the weekends—and they all carried pagers. I asked the manager what was going on, and he just rolled his eyes.

"Oh, honey child, you are precious. It's sort of obvious, don't you think?"

I still didn't get it.

He laughed louder and said, "Let's just put it this way: I'm the madam."

I was shocked. "I can't work in a house of ill repute! I'll finish this weekend, but then I'm out."

The manager was nonplussed. "You can't just break your contract."

"So sue me."

The following Friday they had a new band. I heard later that that very night the cops raided the place and busted everybody in sight. My friends all called to needle me, including my pastor, who'd brought a church group to hear me sing one weekend. "You were playing in a house of ill repute! That could've been you getting busted!"

I tried to comfort him. "Well, nothing happened, thank the Lord. I'm always the last to know 'cause I'm never in the loop!"

Just the latest in a long series of dodged bullets.

– – – – –

I had become a card-carrying member of the entry-level music scene by now, and I hung out at all the right places, where industry honchos and hangers-on congregated. For a while I worked for famed Nashville restaurateur Randy Rayburn at the Sunset Grill, which was kind of the mother ship, where the industry ruling class was generally on display. I connected with a lot of folks as I waited on people there, and I did my best to get my name and face established with friendly showbiz figures.

There was a pecking order in the business, some of it obvious and some of it hidden in the shadows. Superstars and supermanagers were at the top of the food chain, followed by big-shot record execs, producers, and songwriters. Then came the lawyers, agents, and business managers, followed by the administrative and financial class. Finally, bringing up the rear were the people who actually played their instruments onstage and in the studio—the musicians, who seemed to me to have the most thankless role in the whole industry. Every hot player from every small town in the country thought he or she could come to Nashville and make a splash, but the truth was a little more complicated. The city was overrun with brilliant, accomplished musicians, most of whom were playing in bars or at private parties and earning low dollars doing song demos, patiently waiting for someone to notice how great they were.

It seemed a particularly harsh social order, and it got me wondering where I might eventually fall in the hierarchy. I knew it would all rest on my ability to wow people with my stage presence, my voice, and my personality—in other words, did I have the personal attributes to be a star? I wanted it, but honestly, after seeing how much talent there was in my new hometown, I wasn't so sure. I held out hope that the combination of some great original songs, a good band, lots of hard work, and good old-fashioned stick-to-it-iveness could at least get me a shot.

I needed to reach out more and network more; I knew that. And most important, I needed to get some of the right people in my corner. So far, I'd gotten lots of encouragement, but nobody in the upper levels of the Nashville machine had deigned to say, "Let me groom you for a career in music."

I was going to have to dig deeper. I kept knocking on doors, networking, and reaching out to new people, always looking for a half-open door or an opportunity.

I met Bob Wolf, who owned Wolfy's, where all the NHL Nashville Predators players would hang out. Bob had heard us play and liked our stagecraft, so I talked him into giving us a job as the house band at Wolfy's. He and his wife thought I could do more than front a honky-tonk band, and they encouraged me to think about trying other things where my sense of showmanship could be used. His first big idea was a "how-to" reality show about cleaning.

No one else was doing anything like this on television at the time, so I figured, "Why not?" He put up a few bucks, and we started filming some sequences about cleaning techniques and tips and tricks. I'd smile at the camera and say, "Today, we're going to learn about how to take a stain out of the carpet without breaking the bank." And then I'd demonstrate.

The project never went anywhere, but it gave me a little experience and some insight into what it would be like to work on camera. I decided to practice so I'd be ready if and when my big break came around. I visualized the entire world as my television set. When we were playing a set at Wolfy's, I would imagine we were shooting a CMT concert special. Whenever I was cooking by myself or at home, I would imagine I was hosting a cooking show.

One night I remember stopping cold and asking myself,

"Why am I pretending to be doing a cooking show? I'm supposed to be a singer. Or am I?"

It was perhaps the first moment I ever consciously thought about a career path that didn't include music. As I took a hard look at my situation, I saw that many people were multitalented, applying their skills to more than one discipline. I had many interests, too. Maybe my gifts and energies could go in multiple directions.

Would my future be exclusively about music? Or food? Or both?

But it would be my love life that came first.

- - - - - - - - - - -

Lessons for Life and Business

Humility can be hard to come by, and sometimes when it arrives, it hurts. But often you can win by losing and find victory in defeat, even when you feel outgunned. Just remember that two thousand years ago the world was changed forever by a humble man armed only with a simple message of truth, brotherhood, and love.

BLUE RIBBON PUMPKIN BREAD

*B*lue Ribbon Pumpkin Bread goes great with Gigi's Friendship Tea (page 287). The recipe's been in my family since the late 1800s, passed down from my great-great-grandmother. This bread also inspired the pumpkin spice latte cupcake that's added to the menu at Gigi's Cupcakes every fall; it's one of our most beloved recipes.

When I slice this bread it brings back many warm memories—of working at my aunt's elbow, of making my way through recipes with my mom, of laying out a Thanksgiving spread for the whole family. I love it so much I can eat almost a whole loaf in one sitting! (Seriously, I can!)

Put a slab of butter on it and . . . PERFECTION!

INGREDIENTS

3 cups all-purpose flour

2 cups granulated sugar

1 cup brown sugar

2 teaspoons baking soda

1 teaspoon salt

2 teaspoons ground cinnamon

1 teaspoon ground nutmeg

1 teaspoon pumpkin pie spice

1 teaspoon ground ginger

2 cups canned pumpkin puree (or cubed, cooked fresh)

4 large eggs

1 cup canola oil

1 cup chopped pecans

1 teaspoon vanilla extract

1 cup raisins (optional)

• Preheat the oven to 350°F. Grease 2 standard loaf pans.

• In a large bowl, whisk together the flour, granulated sugar, brown sugar, baking soda, salt, and spices.

• Add the pumpkin puree, eggs, oil, and ⅔ cup water.

• Fold in the pecans, vanilla, and raisins (if desired).

• Pour the batter into the prepared pans.

• Bake for 1 hour.

• When a toothpick comes out clean, it's done.

NOT SO HAPPILY EVER AFTER

-- -- -- -- -- -- -- -- -- -- --

A Domestic Adventure

*A*s I motored through my late twenties, I led a robust life, active and energetic, throwing myself into one adventure after another. I'd had my share of garden-variety health problems, but nothing major or life-threatening. I wasn't particularly diligent about diet or fitness, and I spent a lot of long hours working—cleaning houses by day and playing in smoke-filled honky-tonks by night. Grabbing a sandwich here, chugging a coffee there, sneaking a snack whenever I could, and getting by on a minimal amount of sleep, I occasionally found myself worn down.

Even though I'd trained professionally, I'd pushed my voice hard for a decade and had suffered a series of throat problems, infections, fevers, and other ailments. Finally, an ENT ordered my tonsils out, which helped a little. But after that I'd still get mono, or pneumonia, or strep, and the whole system would be on the verge of collapse again.

The real challenge had always been weight control. My appetites and genetics made for a lethal one-two punch for a woman who was intent on slimming down. Over the years I tried many diet strategies and made some half-hearted attempts to modify my behavior, but I always seemed to wind up back where I started.

Frustrated by all this, in the summer of 1999 I decided to go at it hard. I dramatically cut my intake, ruthlessly monitored the caloric value of what I did eat, and forced myself into what became a very unhealthy state. With no real rhyme or reason behind my self-imposed "diet," I grew weak and fell ill. My friends got worried and implored me to go see a specialist. Their pitch was simple: If you're intent on losing a bunch of weight, get a professional to help you.

Which is how I came to meet Ken, a nutritionist at Saint Thomas Hospital, who put me on a sensible, sane, and manageable program to curb my appetite and intake, introduce some fitness concepts to my lifestyle, and reapproach weight loss in a rational, patient way. Pretty soon I looked and felt better, the pounds started coming off, and I began to enjoy a new routine that wasn't pressurized or solely driven by my problematic self-image.

Oh . . . and by the end of the summer I'd fallen in love with Ken.

When he asked me to marry him, I said yes.

– – – – –

Ours was a whirlwind courtship, full of fun evenings and dinners and conversations. We shared a similar worldview and deep religious faith, our senses of humor lined up, and we had similar long-term goals about one day raising a family. All the elements appeared to be in place.

But in truth, it was all happening pretty fast. Ken had been raised in a wealthy home, and his family was always able and willing to help him financially. I did notice just the slightest touch of entitlement in the way he dealt with other people. In retrospect, I should have considered how growing up that way might have affected his attitude toward marriage, especially since he'd decided to marry someone from the other side of the tracks.

I tried to be honest with myself about what was in my heart. Was I truly in love with Ken, or was I merely in love with the *idea* of being in love with Ken? I was certain I was looking to live a big and bold life. For the moment, at least on a superficial level, I thought that could happen with Ken.

But the warning signs continued to pile up. The first time I met his mother, Linda, she looked me up and down with obvious disdain, and in conversation she made it plain that she didn't think I was good enough for her son. I'd heard worse, so I ignored most of her petty little snubs. Despite my misgivings, we set a date—May 1, 2000—and told our friends and relatives.

As the holidays approached, my parents were in town and we went to a big joint-family Christmas dinner at Ken's parents' house, where we all made salted dough ornaments for their Christmas tree. Because everyone was going to get his or her hands covered in dough, I put my brand-new engagement ring in a decorative bowl Linda had on her counter.

Ken was kind of obsessed with this ring and didn't like for me to take it off. Linda could see he was doing a slow burn about this and suggested I wear it around my neck. But I said no, the bowl was fine. Neither Linda nor Ken was happy with this, but I was loose, having fun, and decided not to sweat it. The dinner went well, everyone got along, and we rang in the holiday with a few laughs. I was relieved.

Driving back to my place that evening, I realized I'd left the ring in the bowl. I suggested we go back, but we were already halfway home. I decided to swing by the next day between cleaning jobs and pick it up.

My mom was helping me clean that day. We stopped by Ken's parents' house together. Linda answered the door, all smiles. "Well, this is a nice surprise."

I gave her a hug. "Hi, Linda, sorry to drop in on you, but I left my ring here last night."

"What ring?"

"Remember, I put my engagement ring in the bowl? And you suggested I wear it around my neck?"

She reacted as if she had never heard any of this before. But she made a show of inviting us inside to look for it. We followed her into the kitchen, and I pointed to the decorative bowl on the counter where I'd left the ring just twelve hours earlier. "Right there," I said.

She checked it, and then shrugged helplessly. A mock-scolding look came over her face. "Did you lose that extremely expensive diamond ring? If so, I certainly hope it was insured."

"I'm sure it's around here somewhere. When you find it, please let me know."

We got back in the car, and a few minutes later Ken called. He was furious about the missing ring, and I wondered if Linda had engineered this to teach me a lesson about who was in control in Ken's family.

I called Linda that evening. Her answering machine picked up, so I left a calm, assured message that I knew would get a reaction of some kind.

"Linda," I began sweetly, "just let me know when you decide you're going to give the ring back to me. Hopefully it'll be before I need it for the wedding. In the meantime I guess everyone will just think your son proposed to me without offering a ring."

Before I could sign off she picked up. "You lost the ring because you're irresponsible."

I didn't respond.

She continued. "I found the ring. It was in the dryer. It must have gone in with the linens and dish towels."

"Whatever you say, Linda."

That set her off. "There's something I don't understand about you. A garbage man doesn't drive a Cadillac. Why should somebody who cleans toilets for a living need a rock like that on her hand?"

"Linda, do you understand what you just said to me?"

She didn't miss a beat. "I know exactly what I just said." I thanked her for locating the missing ring and asked her to give it to Ken for me. I had zero interest in seeing that woman again, at least for a little while.

- - - - -

Despite all the flak and static, May 1, 2000, approached. My wedding day was at hand.

I'd done all the planning, and now my mom and aunts were doing all the food. It was great to have so many expert hands to make light of all that work.

My old friend Helen Barnett came and pitched right in, as usual. She tried to apply her staging and showbiz skills to the rehearsal, but Ken was in full "commander" mode, telling everyone what to do and where to stand. After he'd told me when to walk down the aisle, he announced that he had decided to break with tradition in another area. He said to me, "I want to walk down the aisle, too—you know, by myself, with some music. This is my big day, too."

My mom didn't get it. "You mean, like a bride?"

Ken bristled. "No, like a groom."

Since I couldn't come up with a response to this nutty idea, Helen jumped in. "That's a lovely idea, but you're the groom," she said delicately. "You just walk out from the side. This is a young woman's big day, the bride's shining moment."

He shook his head. "It's my big day, too. I'm entitled to as much of the limelight as she is."

Helen continued, "But Ken, you're the *guy*. Wedding days are not about the guy."

He started to boil. I could see a storm coming, so I tried to mediate. "Ken, if you want to walk down the aisle, too, I don't care. Go ahead, walk down the aisle."

But finally, one of his groomsmen said, "Why do you want to be like a chick? Come out from the side, man."

There was an awkward pause, and then all the groomsmen kind of joined in until Ken relented.

"Okay," he murmured. "I'll come out on the side. But this is my big day, too."

Ken's need for control—something I'd seen only small glimpses of during our lightning-fast courtship—was real.

During the rehearsal dinner, Linda got up to make a toast. She said, "When Ken brought this little house cleaner into our home we thought, 'Well, maybe.' And then I saw her toe ring and I thought, 'Well, she looks like she might be a bit of a slut, but if my Ken loves her then we're going to try to love her the best we can.' "

You could have heard a pin drop as she sat back down, smug and self-satisfied. She'd brazenly insulted me. Helen leaned over with real concern in her eyes. She whispered, "Gina, I know it's the day before your wedding and all, but are you sure you want to go through with this?"

After the rehearsal dinner, everyone broke up to go to the bachelor and bachelorette parties. I asked Ken to take my brothers with him, something that seemed pretty standard. But he bristled. "Why would I want to take your brothers with me?"

I was surprised. "Well, they don't know anybody and you could make them feel welcome. I'm taking some of your cousins and friends to my bachelorette party."

He smirked. "This is my last night of freedom. I'm going to be with my friends, not your family."

Everyone on the Butler side was extremely weirded out. Right then something clicked in my head: a big, red, flashing warning light. I took a step back and asked myself one more time, "Do you have any idea what you're doing?" But then I thought, "Who cancels their wedding the night before? That's like something you only see in a movie." But there was no denying the dull ache in my chest—or the fear that was creeping up my spine.

That night, my parents stayed with me. I halfway expected a conversation of some sort, but Mom and Dad mumbled their good nights and padded off to bed. I had given them my bedroom, so I put together a makeshift bed on the living room floor. (I still can't believe I slept on the floor the night before my wedding!)

I cried all night, because I knew in my heart that this was all wrong—none of it felt right. There was no excitement about what the morning would bring. I'd made a terrible mistake, and I knew it.

My dad woke up and heard me crying. He came downstairs and put an arm around me. "Gina, you don't have to do this. I'll go and talk to him."

But I just couldn't quite admit that I'd made such a huge mistake. "No, we'll have a good life together," I assured him. "It'll be fine."

He stared at me long and hard. Finally, he kissed me on the cheek and went back to bed. I absolutely loved him for asking the question, I really did. But a part of me wanted my daddy to take control and make it all right. I longed for him to sweep me up in his big, strong arms and take me away to a place where I'd be safe and loved, just as he'd done when I was a little girl.

The next morning we all went to church and the deed was done. Our families behaved, and we smiled and danced and ate and drank and toasted and hugged and cried.

About 380 people showed up at the West End Church of

Christ, including a hundred or so from out of town—relatives, family friends, and old pals from Quartz Hill. It was a touching turnout of people who wanted to come and support me.

If there was ever a dark omen offered to a bride on her wedding day, it happened to me. My aunt Bennie had lovingly fashioned a tall, multitiered cake in her Texas bakery and carefully transported it to Nashville for my big day.

Just before the reception, as Aunt Bennie was buzzing around setting things up, the delicate cake had inexplicably lost its structural integrity, teetered over, and collapsed in a heap. Unfazed, Bennie and her assistants scrambled to reassemble it as best they could, and somehow they managed to get it ready for the reception.

But the metaphor was inescapable. I was doomed.

- - - - -

We spent our honeymoon at a luxurious hotel in the Bahamas. An hour after we arrived, as I was unpacking my bag, I noticed Ken standing off to one side, critically inspecting my clothes as they came out of my suitcase. He was upset that I hadn't brought more negligees. And things went downhill from there.

We fought nonstop for the entire honeymoon. I couldn't do anything right—my clothes, my hair, the activities I suggested, you name it. I cried the whole time. If we were out walking along the beach, he'd get mad because he thought we needed to be in the room having sex. We met a couple who played ping-pong with us, and halfway through the game he thought something untoward was going on and he got upset. So we abruptly went back to the room, where he flipped out again about how I'd done something wrong.

The trip was a nightmare. When I got home, I told everyone we'd had a delightful time, that the islands were so beautiful, that everything was so romantic. But back in my own bed, I lay awake each night and kicked myself. I was certain I'd made the biggest mistake of my life.

– – – – –

After a few months of marriage, Ken asked me to stop writing with my usual songwriting partners, who all happened to be guys. I tried to reason with him—I'd been writing with some of these guys for five years or more. But Ken was afraid they were all trying to sleep with me. To keep the peace, I reluctantly suspended my writing sessions. But I was in knots trying to figure out how to advance my musical ambitions without interacting with men.

One day I was mopping the kitchen, and he walked in and tramped right across my clean floor. He sat on the couch and stared at me. He clearly had something on his mind. It turned out he'd discovered I'd left my wedding band on the bathroom shelf while I'd been at work cleaning houses. Why would I leave home without my wedding band, unless I was inviting men to come on to me? It never occurred to Ken that with all the chemicals and rubber gloves and wiping and scraping I did, it made perfect sense to leave my jewelry at home.

Oddly, each of Ken's family members had somehow gotten a key to our house. This happened without any discussion, so it surprised me the first few times I went into the kitchen and found his mother standing there. Now, I didn't have any real boundaries with my family, so I didn't buck the system. But Linda would come in as if she were inspecting an army barracks. She'd criticize how I washed his clothes and suggested that maybe she should do his laundry.

One night we were out to dinner with his parents, and Ken said, "Mommy, I really need some new jeans."

I told Ken I'd be happy to pick up some new jeans for him, but the next day I came home and found ten pairs of new jeans on the bed. My mother-in-law was determined to make sure her little boy was taken care of her way, not mine. Today, if people in my world behaved that weirdly, I'd run for the exits.

Ken and I got in the habit of taking walks. One day we were tooling along in Belle Meade and I picked up a stick. Then he picked up a stick. I tapped him on his bum and he tapped me on mine. We repeated this a few times, and I guess I hit him a little too hard with one whack, because without any warning he screamed, "Stop!"

He wound up and whipped his stick across my back. It hurt so bad.

"That's it, no more—you're hurting me!" I yelled. He ripped my stick away, cutting my hand, and then he pushed me so hard that I stumbled off the curb and onto the street.

Things got worse after this incident. For a while, he'd block the doors in our home so I couldn't go from one room to another—and couldn't leave the premises without his okay. One morning we were horsing around and he started getting rough. I wound up with a bruise the size of an apple on my leg. When I begged him to stop, he shoved me away in disgust.

He could see I was scared, so he softened and put his arms around me. I thought he was going to apologize and comfort me, but he didn't. Instead, he looked me right in the eye. "If you ever leave me or my family, I will hunt you down."

Even though he was talking nonsense, I knew what I needed to say at that moment. "I'm not going to ever leave you. I love you."

- - - - -

One fall day in October he and his father went off to a Vanderbilt football game, and I was alone with my thoughts. If I cleaned the house and washed his clothes and made a great dinner and was gracious to his father when they got home, maybe he wouldn't be mean to me that night. As I was cleaning the dining room mirror, I caught sight of myself. I thought, "What's happening to me? Who am I becoming?"

I got a puppy and named him Prancer because he looked like a broken-down reindeer. He was the ugliest, scraggliest little rescue dog you could ever imagine. But we bonded immediately. In the morning he was thrilled to see me. In the evening he couldn't wait to curl up with me. And during the day he dutifully followed me everywhere, loyal and dedicated to being my pal. He even went with me to clean houses.

One day I came home and found him shivering in a corner of the house, shaken up and whimpering. Ken came in from work, and Prancer immediately recoiled, spooked as if he'd seen the devil himself. I looked at the dog and looked at Ken, and caught the tiniest bit of a smile pass across Ken's face. I was ready to put two and two together, but I really didn't want to.

I knew it was time to get out.

- - - - -

That brutal October I began mapping out my escape. If Ken learned I was leaving him, all bets would be off; I couldn't predict what might happen to me if he found out. So I decided to do my homework, get everything ready, and pull the trigger right after Christmas. I called my parents and told them I was leaving Ken and swore them to secrecy.

As the weeks rolled by, I started looking around for a place to live and checked into what I would need to do with our bank accounts and insurance policies. And most important, I started looking for a divorce lawyer I could afford.

All this involved quite a bit of sneaking around. But one night all my best-laid plans blew up in my face. I came in from singing at a gig, and Ken was waiting for me at the kitchen table. He'd found my diary and learned how I'd been looking for apartments.

He glared at me. "How long has it been since you decided to leave me?"

The jig was up. I sighed and joined him at the table. "Quite a while, actually. I can't live with your family. I can't live with you. I want another life, and I want it now."

He told me I wasn't going to get any of his money or property. If I wanted to leave, I could just leave right then. His voice rose in pitch, and it seemed to me he was starting to freak out.

He slipped to the kitchen floor and started crying.

I picked up Prancer and my bag and headed for the door.

From the car I called Linda. "I've left your son tonight," I said, "and I want to tell you I'm afraid for him and for your family."

You know what Linda said to me?

"How dare you leave my son!"

I was through with being a nice daughter-in-law. "He needs help. Help him!"

She started to argue, but I was done. I hung up and blocked her number. I was ready to flush all the crazy out of my life.

— — — — —

My dad and I went back to my house one day while Ken was at work and we moved my stuff out—clothes, keepsakes from the wedding. I left all the beds, furniture, appliances, everything. I never looked back.

I filed for divorce, but Ken initially didn't want to play ball. Six months dragged by until Dale Denny, a lawyer friend from church, said to Ken, "Okay, if you don't give her a divorce, we're taking you to court. We'll pursue you for abuse, neglect, the whole nine yards."

Ken signed immediately, and we wound up with an uncontested divorce. Oddly, he made a last-ditch effort to negotiate shared custody of Prancer—the same poor little dog he'd terrified. Prancer was all mine!

I saw Ken about five years later. He was watching a football game on TV in a sports bar in Hillsboro Village. I was with a girlfriend and we were talking to some guys, and suddenly there he was. I was scared to death, but he came over to say hello and we stepped outside to talk.

"I'm so sorry I hurt you," he said. "I was so horrible to you. I really, really apologize. It was all my fault." It was kind of healing. He said he'd had counseling and he knew his parents were tough. He kept apologizing, until I gave him a little hug and wished him well. I finally had closure.

– – – – –

After my marriage broke up I went on a "getaway trip" to the United Kingdom with my mom, Hazel Lyons, and my pal Wanda Gary. We spent a month tooling around England, Scotland, Wales, and Ireland. I couldn't believe how beautiful and green everything was. Tennessee is lush and verdant, too, but England has its own palette of greens. We saw all the sights, visited a bunch of museums, gobbled up British delicacies, and learned how to drive on the wrong side of the road. I even figured out how to read the London Tube maps well enough to get back to the hotel every day.

One afternoon in York we took a walk after a rainstorm, and I poured my entire heart out to my mother.

"I'm not sure I'm ever going to be the same after all this," I began. "I don't know if I'll ever heal."

My mom put her arm around me and pulled me in close. "It'll get better, I promise. God knows what He's doing. You'll come back from this."

As if on cue, a huge, bright double rainbow appeared overhead, arching high over the city skyline. While we both stared at it openmouthed, a beautiful monarch butterfly floated into view and landed right on my shoulder. We looked at each other and completely cracked up.

"Well," Mom said, "if you were looking for a sign from above, I think you got it!"

It was the perfect diversion after a year in hell—the perfect balm for my abraded soul.

— — — — — — — — — — —

Lessons for Life and Business

Don't get bogged down in the past. Don't let old mistakes, rivalries, and grudges ruin your spirit. Live each day anew, with freshness and optimism, and know that your best days will always be ahead of you—if you make it so.

MAMA'S MANICOTTI

*T*his is my mom's famous recipe. She is Italian, and she loves to make dishes from the old country. Her father, Getulio Nodini's, parents came from northern Italy in the early 1900s, and Mom's strong connection to her roots is reflected in this, one of her favorite old-world recipes. *Mangia!*

INGREDIENTS

$1/2$ pound ground turkey or beef

1 large onion, diced

One (6-ounce) package frozen spinach, thawed and drained

$1^1/4$ cups (10 ounces) low-fat cottage cheese

$1/4$ cup freshly grated Parmesan cheese

1 large egg

1 cup plus $1/2$ cup shredded low-fat mozzarella cheese

Salt and black pepper

12 manicotti shells

4 cups spaghetti sauce, divided

- Preheat the oven to 350°F.

- Brown the meat with the onion and drain.

- Add the spinach, cottage cheese, Parmesan cheese, egg, 1 cup mozzarella cheese, and salt and pepper to taste. Mix well and set aside.

- In a large pot, boil the manicotti shells until al dente.

- Rinse the manicotti shells and pat dry with a paper towel.

- Into a 9 x 13-inch baking dish, pour 2 cups spaghetti sauce.

- Stuff the shells with the meat mixture and place side by side in the baking dish on top of the sauce.

- Pour the remaining 2 cups sauce over the shells and sprinkle with the remaining ½ cup mozzarella cheese.

- Bake for about 40 minutes, until golden brown.

DREAMS DIE HARD

- - - - - - - - - - - - - - - -

A Girl's Got to Know Her Limitations . . .
Or Does She?

*N*ow it was time to get everything back on track and start a new chapter. Prancer and I moved out to Bellevue and got settled in a little apartment. I threw myself into music, but now with a slightly different compass heading. I was writing more now, trying to find my own voice and point of view. I knew I could sing and cover songs made famous by other artists, but it was becoming more and more obvious that I needed to perfect a unique style and presence. The world already had a Linda Ronstadt and a Patty Loveless and a Reba McEntire; the question was, did it need a Gina Butler? The clock was ticking for me now, and I had to step up my efforts if I wanted a meaningful career in music.

Around this time, my band became the center of my universe. We'd pile into a van and head out two weekends a month, going wherever I could arrange gigs—Tennessee, Kentucky,

Alabama, even all the way to Texas and Oklahoma. We averaged about seventy-five shows a year traveling around like that—four-hour gigs, four sets a night.

Since we usually hit the road early on Friday, I'd ask my Friday and Saturday clients if I could clean on Thursday or Monday. I had a good rep with my customers, and they knew I'd always deliver quality and would do what I said I'd do, so they generally agreed. Even the toughest clients—the picky, never-satisfied ones—got over their initial resistance because they knew I was diligent and could be trusted to make good.

But as much as I loved singing and as badly as I wanted to make it in the music industry, sometimes I'd be out on the road somewhere and I'd honestly find myself wondering what I was doing. As I darted in and out of town, I had to juggle my expanding cleaning business, and I had virtually no personal life at all. I didn't date for about a year and a half after the divorce. I wanted to cleanse myself and I wanted to grieve, but mostly I was just afraid. Afraid of Ken, afraid of what would come next, afraid I'd never make it in the music business . . . just afraid.

In the middle of this transition, my mom was diagnosed with breast cancer. The news hit me like a truck; the thought of losing her was paralyzing, incomprehensible, overpowering. There was an immediate rush of information about her medical situation—treatment schedules and options, doctors and opinions, decisions about hospitals and home care. I dove right in and tried to help as best I could long-distance.

Also at that time, I became a member of the Woodmont Hills Church and was immediately welcomed into the large, warm, and friendly congregation. Everybody tried to make me feel at home from my very first visit—one of the things I love about church life—but I was pretty depressed.

My mom and dad could sense something was up with me. They could tell my spirit had been broken. Mom couldn't recall ever seeing me so down in the dumps; I'd always been relentlessly upbeat and optimistic. She convinced me to come visit her in Texas, where they had moved in 2000. I was thrilled to see that her medical progress was exemplary, and that she was looking at a happy outcome. I, on the other hand, had pretty much curled up into a ball. I guess I was finally taking the time to grieve about everything.

I spent a lot of time on my own, holed up in my room. I had trouble eating and sleeping, and I cried at the drop of a hat. I lost fifteen pounds, and for the first and only time in my life I was prescribed depression medicine. My doctor didn't think I was going to kill myself, but she did wonder if perhaps I'd unintentionally starve myself to death. I was so sick. But after a month I felt pretty stable again and didn't need the meds anymore.

Being with family and feeling protected after living in such a raw and exposed way for so long really calmed the situation, smoothed out some of the wrinkles, and helped me get my feet back on the ground. I needed to regain my strength so I could dive back into my little world.

- - - - -

Music is a fascinating, amazing, inspiring thing to me. When I think about all the songs that appear on the soundtrack of my life, my heart is indescribably full. I'm humbled by all the wondrous gifts of melody and poetry that so many singers and writers and pickers and producers have given to people. And in my heart of hearts I'm overwhelmed with pride and gratitude for having been a part of it all for so long.

But Nashville is just like any other place, a city full of the best and worst that humanity has to offer. Over the years I got to know lots of people on both sides of that divide, and I believe for sure that there are far more good guys than bad guys. But the bad guys make for particularly good copy. People always say Hollywood's corrupt, but I don't think it can hold a candle to Nashville. The country music business is full of some of the biggest hypocrites on earth. Everything is couched in the sweet, honeyed vernacular of the good ol' boy tradition, and it can be hard to tell who's a liar and who isn't. The real players are expert at covering their tracks and making sure their public profiles remain pristine, because it's important to support the broad concept that country music is just "one big happy family." So-called family values and good old-fashioned Christianity loom large in that happy family's legend.

I get that we're all a little bit good and a little bit bad. That's human nature. And staying on the "good path" requires some work—keeping our commitments to God, our family, and our fellow citizens is not always easy. But following through, doing what we say we'll do, being a person of our word, behaving honestly and forthrightly, treating other people with respect and kindness—these actions provide important insights into our character and often determine how credible we are. Besides the fact that God is watching us, that credibility—or lack thereof—is what other people use to take our measure.

I found the mix of business and religion to be a little complicated: Can a person live unethically for six days a week and then

LEFT: My second birthday, with my chocolate train cake. Can you tell we always celebrated goodness surrounding us?! I learned the language of love at an early age.
RIGHT: My family at a wedding . . . gotta love the late '70s!

LEFT: My dad and I trying to give one of our potbellied pigs his medicine.
RIGHT: Eight years old, and surrounded by California poppies. Whenever I'm stressed, I close my eyes and go back to this time in my life.

LEFT: My grandma Edrie Lanig, who was so adventurous! RIGHT: My favorite picture from my childhood. As a kid, I truly wanted to be Wonder Woman!

LEFT: My fifteenth birthday—with a coconut cake made from Great Aunt Birdie's recipe that my mom made for me every year. RIGHT: The first time I sang on stage by myself, singing "What Child Is This?" I was hooked!

Trying out with a new band in Pear Blossom, California. Can you tell I'm a little nervous? Gotta love the shorts!

Learning how to play guitar during summer vacation at Lake Powell.

My early days singing with the Wild Silver Band.

The first time I saw my name in lights! The Riverside Casino in Laughlin, Nevada.

My first night at Robert's Western World in downtown Nashville, my all-time favorite place to play.

A new vacuum cleaner for Gigi's Cleaning Company. I was hard on vacuums, and went through a couple dozen before I learned to love and depend on Bissel vacuum cleaners, which worked the best and the longest. I really should have been their spokesperson . . . maybe I still can be one day!

TOP LEFT: The day before I opened my first store. My sweet dog, Prancer, was always by my side. He lived for sixteen years. TOP RIGHT: The first summer Gigi's Cupcakes was open. I was so happy. My mom and I had just created the Orange Dreamsicle cupcake! I was about to frost some for the first time. RIGHT: The first wedding I catered for Gigi's Cupcakes. BOTTOM: Signing the first franchise contract with Alan Thompson, my partner.

TOP LEFT: With Brad Harlan and the cupcakes that Taylor Swift ordered as thank-you gifts for radio staff. They were red velvet with white chocolate letters TS. How thankful I was that she chose Gigi's Cupcakes.

TOP RIGHT: Our original dream team taking Gigi's Cupcakes on the road.

RIGHT: Aunt Bennie Lee and I do a cake-making video at the store. I loved working with her. She is a true treasure. BOTTOM: Kendel Skye started traveling with me at an early age . . . this is how we rolled!

LEFT: Before her first birthday, Kendel Skye was already pushing the brand! RIGHT: With Kendel Skye in Seaside, Florida, one of our all-time favorite places to chill.

LEFT: One of my favorite places: Opryland Hotel. Once a year we spend a night at the hotel, look at the Christmas lights, and enjoy a little "special time." *(Liz Ross Cruse)* RIGHT: Introducing Kendel Skye to how the business works. Who wouldn't buy cupcakes from this little darling?

My celebration photo. When you have sprinkles and cupcakes all around you, how could you not be happy? *(Ashley Hylbert/Gigi's Cupcakes)*

Doing a cooking demonstration. *(Ashley Hylbert/Gigi's Cupcakes)*

Some of my favorite people: Bud Schaetzle, my co-writing genius, and Tony Brown, producer extraordinaire.

Kendel Skye at five years old. Such a sweet, magical age!

try to even it all out on Sunday morning? During the workweek on Music Row you could get the runaround mentally, financially, or ethically by someone who'd go out and behave badly on Saturday night—but on Sunday morning would grab a pew, all shined up like a choirboy, pious and wholesome. Many find their absolution this way, but in my book this kind of shortcutting just makes for a cultural Christian—a show pony who's only in it for the superficial benefits that accrue to "good churchgoers." I guess we're all guilty of being cultural Christians now and then. But I believe real faith opens your heart to God and changes your life, taking you to a place where you can serve His message of love and brotherhood. It might take your whole life to fully embrace this and become a disciple of His truth. I'm certainly no angel. I've colored outside the moral and ethical lines plenty of times. But I've tried to correct my behavior and choose a route that would get me where I wanted to go without hurting other people.

This "happy family" culture I tried to crack was a hypermasculine whirligig. Amid intense competition, nonstop stress, and the scrutiny of demanding artists, the media, and corporate masters, many of the industry leaders I met exorcised their demons in a variety of ways. They drank, smoked, cheated on their wives and girlfriends, treated people like garbage, stole other people's songs, ideas, and money, and elevated their ambition above all else. They usually got away with it, because everybody was playing more or less the same game. My friends in other businesses assured me it was the same everywhere, but I took particular exception to it in the music biz because creativity and expression had always been so precious to me, almost sacred. It was disillusioning and heartbreaking to learn that the captains of this industry I'd so longed to be a part of were often found to be so lacking in principle.

The smartest thing to do in life, of course, is to steer clear of these types of people. Just avoid them and go about your business with people who see things the way you do. This is a great strategy—unless you're trying to make it in country music, which is built upon one-on-one relationships, from songwriters to producers to managers to executives to artists. And every one of these relationships begins with a sit-down, where a couple people try to get to know one another to see if their creative instincts align in a way that might be useful. These encounters are driven by the hope that sparks might fly, that something new and memorable—and valuable—will follow. It's impossible to weed out the bad apples, because so many of them are supremely talented!

When I started working to advance my career beyond playing with the Wild Silver boys, I networked with some accomplished and influential folks in town. What I saw and heard got me wondering whether or not I was willing to do what was necessary to "make it."

For example, at one point I set up a writing session with an award-winning songwriter. We met, hit it off right away, and dove into a songwriting session. Before too long we'd come up with something that sounded promising to me. We got to the end of the session and started looking at our calendars to find another time to finish the song.

"I think it's going pretty good, don't you?" he said.

I was excited. "I really do, thank you. This has been great."

Then he said, "Well, then come on over here and kiss me."

I was gobsmacked. How unprofessional! Plus, this dude looked like a potato in blue jeans and boots. I could not have been more repulsed. "What in the name of all that is holy are you talking about?"

He bristled. "Do you want to finish this song or not?"

"Sure I do, but I'm not kissing you."

He shrugged and got up to leave. "Well, I guess we're not going to finish the song then." He packed up his guitar and kind of looked sideways at me as he headed for the door.

Then I got it. "Wait a minute. Are you saying that the only reason you wrote a song with me is so you could have sex with me?"

He sighed as he stepped out the door. "Basically, yeah. 'Cause you're not that talented."

Wow. Classic.

I was furious. What a humiliating, demeaning, inhuman experience.

Unfortunately, I wound up meeting a whole bunch more guys like that songwriter, and many of them were even more influential than he was. Multiplatinum producers, record company executives, music publishers, songwriters, guys who'd been elected to the Country Music Hall of Fame, instrumentalists and pickers who'd influenced everyone from Patsy Cline to the Beatles—dirty old men, dirty young men, dirty dogs all.

One guy—whose house I started to clean right after his wife had their first child!—offered to get me work if I'd be willing to perform certain unmentionable acts upon his body. And there were a dozen or more other propositions of sex-for-advancement that I turned down.

I didn't say anything about it. I didn't tell anyone. I guess I was scared of losing what little I had. I know now, of course, that these guys were probably afraid, too—afraid that they might be outed in front of their families and coworkers and fellow "Christians."

It was hard then—as now—to swim upstream in that environment. There's always too much at stake for the abusers, and they tend to be fierce in protecting their interests. And despite recent events, nobody should get comfortable or harbor any illusions that the problem has been fixed. The kind of sexism and harassment I experienced is alive and well, and has been visited upon countless other women. Yes, the monster's been exposed and maybe weakened a bit, but it has been rampaging throughout the entire entertainment industry for years, and we haven't yet driven a stake through its heart.

I calculate that ninety percent of the young female artists who arrive in Nashville with a dream to sing country music can make it only if (1) they're crazy talented and undeniable (which most of us aren't); (2) they show up with a bag of money from an investor or their dad; (3) they have a close friend or relative who'll pave the way for them; or (4) they get romantically involved with somebody important.

I'd apparently come up empty in all four categories.

I just didn't know what to do about it yet.

- - - - -

Lest you think Music City was a vast wasteland populated by horrible people, let me reassure you, there were plenty of good guys who knew how to treat a girl right.

One of my favorite cleaning clients was guitar hero Lee Roy Parnell, who—in addition to being a world-class musician and a one-of-a-kind gunslinger—was a true gentleman, always kind and helpful and generous, a pleasure to work for. And superstar record producer Tony Brown became a close friend, showing me that you can live by the Golden Rule no matter what happens to you. Tony's work with George Strait, Reba McEntire, Wynonna, Lyle Lovett, the Mavericks, Vince Gill, Brooks & Dunn, Steve Earle, Patty Loveless, and Trisha Yearwood inspired me for many years and transformed the entire industry, and now I'm lucky enough to have his perspective and years of wisdom in my corner.

There were enough good guys to offset the bad apples, and that helped keep me going.

– – – – –

One night I was playing at Tootsie's, passing the tip jar around for peanuts. I thought, "I'm singing other people's songs because nobody wants to hear my songs, I'm dealing with jerk club owners, I'm well into my thirties, and I'm getting my butt pinched by drunk tourists." I paid everyone after the show, and I went home with $45 in my pocket after spending the evening working my tail off.

I suddenly got it: This wasn't going to happen for me. I wasn't going to make it as a singer. The enormity of it overwhelmed me. As I drifted off to sleep, I decided to see if I felt the same way in the morning.

And sure enough, bright and early the next day I had reached a calm, peaceful conclusion: I was done. I needed to start thinking about moving on. Although it was a painful decision in some ways, I knew it was time. I was like a Triple-A ballplayer who never got to the big leagues. And there's a certain nobility in being able to recognize when it's time to quit.

But even though I felt cleansed, after I told the band and my friends and the handful of people I knew and cared about in the music business, I hit a low point. I felt like a failure, a broken-down country singer with no future, no money, no college education, no business, nothing. A loser. I'd tried so hard and worked so hard. I'd endured constant criticism, searing insults, personal abuse, outright bullying, and heartrending condescension. I'd chased my dream the way I'd been taught, but I'd come up short.

Music had been the center of my existence for more than a decade. Now I had to go out and find the rest of my life. Little did I know that what would happen next would change my life forever—along with the lives of everyone I love.

- - - - - - - - - - -

Lessons for Life and Business

Whether you're a big-time CEO or a workaday house cleaner, treat people kindly and with respect. Because the lowly house cleaner might just become your CEO one day— and I promise he or she will remember.

APPLE BROWN BETTY

I love baking pies and cobblers more than anything. And baking with fresh fruit is a real joy! Despite what you may think at first blush, this recipe is delicious and healthy.

When I flew the coop from California and landed in Nashville, I craved the taste of home. So I would bake this and the whole house would smell of apples, home, and love. It was the perfect remedy for my homesickness. The aromas took me back to a time and place I cherished—a crisp fall day in the High Desert, when I'd run into the fragrant kitchen from school and help myself to a bowl of Apple Brown Betty and a warm hug from my mom.

Man, it doesn't get much better than this!

INGREDIENTS

4 Rome apples, peeled, cored, and sliced

4 Granny Smith apples, peeled, cored, and sliced

3 teaspoons ground cinnamon, divided

$1/2$ cup granulated sugar

1 cup all-purpose flour

1 cup brown sugar

$1/2$ teaspoon ground nutmeg

$1/2$ cup butter (softened in the microwave for 12 seconds)

$1/4$ teaspoon salt

$1^1/3$ cups old-fashioned rolled oats

- Preheat the oven to 350°F. Grease a 9 x 13-inch baking dish.

- In a bowl, mix together the apples, 1 teaspoon of the cinnamon, granulated sugar, and ½ cup water. Set aside.

- In a separate bowl, mix together the flour, brown sugar, remaining 2 teaspoons cinnamon, nutmeg, butter, salt, and oats with your fingers until crumbly.

- Place the apple mixture in the prepared baking dish.

- Spread the crumbly mixture over the apples.

- Bake for about 35 minutes, until bubbly.

BOUNCING BACK

- - - - - - - - - - - - - - - -

New People and New Ideas

*O*nce I stopped performing and focused on the expansion of Gigi's Cleaning Company, I had some extra time on my hands to get back in touch with my curious, philosophical side.

To be frank, I was feeling a little lost and sorry for myself. My dream was gone, my husband was gone, and nothing had worked out the way I'd hoped. My family and friends didn't really know what to say, so I turned to the Bible, which I hadn't read much in adulthood. It felt like I was reconnecting with an old friend, and the deeper I dove back into scripture, the more I realized that the answers were right in front of me. Like a lot of people who go through tumultuous change, I had asked, "Why me, Lord?" But humility comes hard, and I knew in my bones that I was just another of God's children going through life's ups and downs.

I revisited Joyce Meyer, a powerful motivational speaker who consistently encouraged women. Her insights about how to think positively reflected my Christian beliefs and resonated with me. Whenever I'd feel low or down on myself, I'd pop in a Joyce Meyer CD and get a quick fix of optimism and hope.

I also read everything I could get my hands on about how to become both a better human being and a better business-person. I loved *The One Minute Manager* by Ken Blanchard and Spencer Johnson, and Michael Gerber's *The E-Myth*, which is all about running small businesses, micromanaging, and the ups and downs of doing everything yourself. Management books, biographies about successful people, business books—I soaked them all up. These thinkers expanded my world a little bit and helped me look beyond the horizon.

- - - - -

Although I could tell you all about the virtues of having a degree from the School of Hard Knocks, deep down I'd always been sensitive about my lack of formal education. I'd always feared that I was wasting my life cleaning houses for a living. Up until this point, I don't think I fully respected what I'd built, because I was always reaching for something I thought was more glam-orous. But now that I was focused fully on the cleaning busi-ness, I felt a twinge of pride, and I started taking my business more seriously than I ever had before. And I had to decide just where I wanted to steer it.

Gigi's Cleaning Company gave me the freedom to start re-creating myself. And if I was going to clean houses for the rest of my life, then I wanted my company to be the best in the busi-ness. I zeroed in on a couple of basic targets. I would do more marketing and take on more clients, which I'd been reluctant to do for a long time. When I'd played in the band, my attention was divided, and I'd only had so much time. Now I could do more.

Taking on more clients meant I'd need more hands on deck. I'd have to hire some help. Now, you meet all kinds of folks in the cleaning business, and there's usually a lot of turnover. But I found that most of the people I hired turned out to be clever, personable individuals who might have just made a few mistakes along the way. I thought Gigi's Cleaning Company could be a lifeline for other people to reinvent themselves, just as I was doing. I enjoyed helping someone who might need a leg up, and I believed that good deeds and good intentions would ultimately lead to positive outcomes for us all.

With this in mind, I hired some girls to work with me who had pretty broken lives. Some were recently off drugs, some had been abandoned, and some were just desperate to make a few dollars. They reported to me, a young woman who understood their situations, and they were free from the monotony of sitting in a claustrophobic office working for a bad boss.

Together, we were going to be the best house cleaners we could be. I would train each staff member personally. I'd instruct her as to what equipment we used, what chemicals we chose and how we prepared them, which particular materials and surfaces needed special care, and how to thread the needle with demanding clients who could be particular, picky, or just plain rude. One at a time, each new girl would go out and work with me for three or four weeks. We'd clean together and interact with the clients, and I'd get her all settled in and used to the GCC routine. Finally, I'd send her off with her own list of houses to clean. Then I'd hire another person and do it all again. Eventually I built up a five-woman crew that could comfortably manage about eighty-five houses a week.

I was always counseling the girls and trying to keep them on the straight and narrow—whether it was with men, drugs, alcohol, or anything else. I found it ironic that my topsy-turvy life would wind up being an inspiration for them; from their perspective, I'd set my own troubles aside and scratched my way to respectability and independence.

I found that I was finally at peace with where I was in life, and I was finally happy with who I was becoming.

– – – – –

I continued to add interesting and colorful clients to my cleaning roster: music people, bankers, doctors, lawyers, real estate tycoons, and businesspeople.

I was referred to a family who had just moved from Pennsylvania to a big house on the lake out in Hendersonville. The parents were both financial executives, and their fourteen-year-old daughter was a musical prodigy who could play, sing, and write like a seasoned pro. Her name was Taylor Swift.

Taylor was a friendly kid, and when I'd show up to clean we'd chitchat a little as she sat on her bed practicing her guitar or working on a new song.

One day she played "Teardrops on My Guitar" and I was floored. She had it all—a great voice, songwriting talent, loads of presence, real star power. I knew that she was going to that place that I'd tried to reach for so long before falling short—she was going to live out my lifelong dream. And I was tickled for her. She was a determined young woman with talent and vision, and I have taken great delight in watching her go on to dominate pop charts all over the world.

Happily, we would cross paths a few years later, after she'd become a superstar and I'd begun my next adventure. Taylor lived in a high-rise right across the street from the flagship Gigi's Cupcakes shop and was a customer from the very beginning. She was especially fond of my Scarlett's Red Velvet cupcake. She'd order about 750 cupcakes every year to give as gifts to the radio guys who came to Nashville for the annual Country Radio Seminar, and we arranged for them to be hand-delivered to hotels all over town.

After watching Taylor win every award in the business, sell millions of records, and break every box office record out there, I could still see the wide-eyed but resolute fourteen-year-old girl practicing in her bedroom, filling up spiral notebooks with lyrics, and dreaming of a storybook life. What a wonderful thing to have your dreams come true!

– – – – –

One day I got a call from a guy named Brad Harlan, who did some work for a high-profile music client he preferred not to name on the phone. He needed a new cleaning service and invited me to visit his boss's house and give him a bid.

I drove out to a massive new 10,000-square-foot mansion a few miles outside of town and met Brad for the first time. We hit it off immediately, kick-starting a rare and wonderful camaraderie that would wind through other jobs and other cities over the next decade, surviving all sorts of ups and downs. Today,

Brad remains one of the best friends I've ever had, someone I love wholly and unreservedly. But more on that later.

I took the job. Brad's client was a multiplatinum Grammy winner. This particular person didn't want a lot of people trooping through her home, though, so I'd go alone to work at her place twice a week for about five hours each day. She was on the road most of the time, so Brad and I usually had the place to ourselves. We built a very special friendship in five-hour segments. We'd put on records and dance and sing, and I found that Brad liked to tell stories and gossip and chitchat as much as I did. More important, we had a lot of experiences in common.

Brad's client had a modest-size entourage that kept their boss's world running smoothly, and some of her people liked things done a certain way. For instance, I was given a detailed lesson on how to place pillows on the beds, which perfumes to spray on which pillows, the number of sprays, and so on. I thought it was a bit much, but hey, I was getting paid so I went with it, eager to please.

The house was well appointed and beautifully maintained, and personally she was a clean and organized individual, which made my job a pleasure. Some clients were out-and-out pigs, which made basic housecleaning more like a toxic waste dump cleanup effort. But she had it together, everybody got along with everybody else, and things just sailed along for a few months.

One day I showed up for work and Brad informed me that later in the day a TV crew would be filming the house for a TV show. The house had been recently renovated, with a beautiful new living room that featured a massive four-by-ten-foot coffee table. The table sported an array of spiritually oriented knickknacks, all carefully arranged around a huge flower bouquet. Next to the flowers there was a three-inch trinket—one of her favorite pieces. I knew the magnificent room would be a visual centerpiece of the TV shoot, so I went the extra mile and spent eight solid hours going over everything with a fine-tooth comb, making sure it was spotless, gleaming, and picture-perfect.

After I finished and was taking my cleaning supplies to my truck, Brad ran out of the house after me. His boss had just gotten home and the TV crew was setting up. I was kind of expecting a pat on the back, but he looked a little concerned. The owner was not so happy about how some things were put back after our cleaning.

Brad hesitated. "One item on the coffee table is not in its proper place."

"I took everything off the coffee table to polish it. Did I forget to put it back?"

Brad squirmed a little, as if he knew how crazy his next words would sound. "No, you put everything back. But one thing is a couple of inches to the right of where it's supposed to be. And she's not too happy about it."

I'd learned that Brad had a good sense of humor, and thought maybe he was joking. "Maybe she could slide it over a couple of inches?"

Brad shook his head firmly. It was no joke. "Yeah, she could, but that's not the point. She instructed me to let you know this is not acceptable."

I flashed red-hot and started back toward the house. But Brad stopped me. "No, no, no . . . don't go back in there."

I took a couple of deep breaths, then lit into him. "Number one, I just busted my hump getting ten-thousand square feet ready to be photographed. Number two, I have a suggestion of another place where she can stick it. And number three—I quit!"

From my perspective, clients could be "fussy," "picky," and "demanding," but sometimes I felt I needed to draw the line.

So that was my last day. I reminded Brad we'd always be friends, and in a prescient moment I jokingly suggested that maybe one day I'd open a restaurant or a bakery and he might want to come and work for me—two predictions that would ultimately come true!

This musician now loves Gigi's Cupcakes, and I continue to be a huge fan of hers—the emotions of that day seem to have long disappeared into the fog of history. But I think of this story and chuckle every time she hits town and orders cupcakes.

– – – – –

Most of our clients were terrific, but some were slightly eccentric, and a handful could be condescending and just outright abusive. I'd developed a thick skin over the years, and to keep my employees sane I drilled into them the reminder that every day our work took us into someone else's personal, private space, and we had to be prepared for our clients to be nitpicky and occasionally insufferable.

But sometimes they pushed me too far. I worked for a quiet, serious couple who had a beautiful home in Brentwood. All went well for a few months, even though they seemed a little lacking in the personality department. I'd never get more than a perfunctory greeting, and their attitude screamed, "You're just the help."

One day I found a chunk of dried cat poop on their main staircase. They evidently hadn't wanted to pick it up themselves, so they'd just stepped around it every day, letting it slowly harden, its noxious fluids leaking into their carpet and staining it. I asked the wife about it.

She snarled, "That's what we pay you for."

Still trying to be patient and helpful, I pointed out the damage that was being done and suggested that maybe they should pick the poop up between my visits. "Maybe your kids could pitch in a little. Chores are good for building character."

"My children don't do that kind of work." She sniffed. "That's your job. If you don't like it, you can quit."

I didn't like it. So I quit.

I worked for another couple for a few weeks—until they asked me to join them in a threesome. I quit them, too.

I think the worst clients, though, weren't the ones who were demanding or fussy. It was the ones who felt entitled and superior, who were condescending and cruel, that rankled me. There were a couple of situations that stuck with me, if only because they confirmed my beliefs about how we're supposed to treat one another.

I had a single, fortysomething client named Marlene who was an Ivy League grad and the head of a company, very smart and accomplished. I cleaned her gorgeous home in Green Hills for ten years. Although she could be picky, I thought for the longest time that she and I enjoyed a basic level of mutual respect. I mean, I wasn't running a huge corporation like she was, but I thought she at least could see I was building my small business and was worthy of her regard.

One morning I was dusting her den while she sat on the couch reading the paper. She seemed to be checking me out as I worked, peering over the top of the paper and making mental notes.

She asked if I was seeing anyone "socially."

"You mean, am I dating anyone?" I asked. "No, not really."

She lowered her newspaper and considered this for a long moment. "I was thinking of setting you up with a guy at my company."

This was unlike her. But I was intrigued. "Wow, thank you, Marlene," I said. "Tell me more."

"Well," she said, "at first I thought you'd find him attractive and he would probably think you're pretty."

I smiled. "Sounds like a good start."

She wrinkled up her nose a little. "But he's an accomplished executive. I'm not sure you're interesting enough for him. He's very white collar and you're probably too blue collar for him. So I guess as I'm thinking this through it probably wasn't a very good idea to begin with."

And she raised her newspaper and went back to reading. I was shocked but wasn't quite sure how to express it. I puttered around with my Swiffer for a moment before responding. "Marlene, let me ask you: What does it matter? I work hard and I own my own business. If he's really a good businessman he would respect that."

She sighed behind the paper. "Well, honey, maybe he'd want you to clean for him. But I'm guessing he's looking for a more educated woman. You know, for the sake of his social life and his future children."

And then, finished with her paper, she got up to leave the room. On her way out, she paused at a bookcase, swiped it with a finger, and smiled sweetly at me. "Looks like you missed a spot."

I left that day feeling pretty degraded and hurt. Of course, I wondered why she had even brought it up in the first place. Had it been a legitimate effort to help me? Or a twisted power trip to put me in my place? Or had she just not been thinking? I'm sure I've said unkind things in my life without really meaning to, but I hope I never rained on anyone's parade as hard as she did on mine that day.

The feeling stuck with me forever. But it also reminded me of why I try to build people up and use positive words. It's important to watch our tongues, for harsh words scald and scar. I keep a carved wood block on my kitchen counter that says, "Lord, keep your arm around my shoulder and your hand over my mouth." I read it every morning and remind myself to watch my tone. I always thought the book of Proverbs really nailed it: "A soft answer turneth away wrath: but grievous words stir up anger."

I continued to work for Marlene until I stopped cleaning houses. The subject never came up again. But after I launched my next venture, I secretly hoped that one morning as she was sitting on that couch paging through her morning paper, she'd pause to read all about the success of Gigi's Cupcakes—and the exciting new company's founding CEO, who'd come from nothing to make her mark in the business world.

— — — — —

One of the oddest encounters began when one of my clients decided to "help" one of my girls. I'd hired a troubled young woman named Sally, who had two little daughters and no man in the picture, a recovering addict who was fighting like crazy to pull her life together and be a good mother. Sally was a little rough around the edges, but she had a good heart. She was kind of timid and fragile, and she seldom interacted with the clients directly.

One day Sally and I were cleaning a mansion when the owner, an old-money dowager, returned from a trip to the farmers' market. I was working in the living room when I heard Sally's voice rising in the kitchen. "No, no. I don't want them, thank you."

But apparently the old gal was on a mission. She'd bought a flat of tomatoes and picked out all the good ones and was now trying to fob the janky leftovers off on Sally. To her chagrin, Sally had recoiled from the rancid tomatoes, which were turning moldy in spots and looked wholly unappetizing.

The woman pressed on. "I'm sure you can trim around the bad parts, my dear. They shouldn't go to waste."

But Sally was getting panicky at the thought of even handling these nasty vegetables. "No, thank you, ma'am . . . no, thank you."

The lady wasn't used to being countermanded by her staff.

"Don't be stupid, child. When your betters are trying to help you, be grateful and accept their charity."

Sally had no idea how to handle this situation. The woman did not intend to be denied and it was turning ugly.

I decided it was time to step in. I took the flat of leftover tomatoes and handed them back. "I'm sure you think you're doing something nice here, but Sally doesn't want them, ma'am."

She pushed them back at me. "Then you take them. Your kind can always use them."

"My kind doesn't eat spoiled food."

She was icy. "There's no reason to be so ungrateful."

"Let me spell it out for you: Nobody wants your rotten tomatoes."

The old woman drew herself up to her full height. "How dare you!"

But I was on a roll. "There's a verse in the Bible about how God wants us to give each other our firstfruits, the best fruits of our garden—which is what we've been giving you and your family every Wednesday for the past year. If this is the best you can do in return, I think you should find yourself another house cleaner."

And we left her sputtering on her front porch.

- - - - -

During this time, my love life wasn't going very well. A year out from my divorce I'd decided it was time to dip a toe back in the pond—and then I quickly dove in with all my clothes on. I became a serial dater. I went kind of crazy. Unfortunately, most of the guys I was interested in weren't interested in me, so all I managed to do was flail around trying to find some basic chemistry with a series of creeps and local Gomers. In retrospect, I probably had no business getting involved with any of them, but at least I was out there making an effort.

I don't know what I was looking for. Some people date because they don't want to sit around the house, and some people date because they're looking for a partner. All I knew was that I was single, I didn't have a child, and I wanted to get out and live a little. Of course, deep down I was looking for a nice man. But at that moment, if a guy had a dimple in his chin, all his teeth, a job, and a good line or two, I'd give him a shot.

Each time, ever the optimist, I started out believing it was possible that sparks could fly. But five minutes into a first date, I could tell every time when they wouldn't. I went through the motions anyway, thinking that maybe a new friendship would come out of the experience. And some of my dates did become good friends; others I set up with other women. In truth, I just liked the process of getting to know people.

Not everything had to lead to romance, and I kept at it, but after a while I decided I'd rather be by myself for a time. I'd gone back into the dating game with an open mind but hadn't really connected with anyone in a lasting way. At the moment, there didn't seem to be much point in playing the game or putting myself in a vulnerable situation, as I had so many times before. Was there a Mr. Right out there for me somewhere?

Soon I'd have a chance to answer that question.

– – – – –

As Gigi's Cleaning Company expanded, I bought my first little house, off of Edmondson Pike in Nippers Corner. I was so proud of myself. I could finally afford a nice SUV so I could haul all my stuff around. Bills were paid. I had great credit. I had a little bit of savings. Overall, I was doing pretty well.

My brother Randall watched me pull it all together and was very supportive. He suggested I talk to Clement Pepe, a life coach he knew who he thought could help me. Clement and I would get on the phone and discuss whatever challenges happened to be in front of me—sometimes business, sometimes personal. He offered me one of the best perspectives I ever heard, a business truism I still apply to this day: "Gigi, doing the hard thing first always makes your life easy. Doing the easy thing first always makes your life harder."

So whenever I had an important choice or decision to make, I'd run it through that filter.

"Well," I'd ask myself, "is this going to be hard?"

I'd answer, "Yeah, it probably will."

"Okay, then go for it—it will all be downhill after this."

As 2007 dawned, I was doing well, having fun with my friends, and working hard. I was comfortably walking a righteous path, applying my faith to my daily life, and striving to better myself however I could—as a person, a daughter, a friend, a boss, and a businesswoman. A lot of the puzzle pieces were fitting together in ways they hadn't just a few short years ago. I was really enjoying my life.

One night in July my girlfriend Ami Kerr and I went to a Nashville Sounds minor-league baseball game, and afterward we went to Tootsie's to hang out and listen to some music. I had fond memories of playing Tootsie's; it was a good place to relax and decompress, and the best for people-watching.

That night the band was great and the beer was cold, and after a while I got up and headed for the ladies' room. As I threaded my way through the crowd, I noticed a guy sitting at the bar staring right at me. And he had a dimple in his chin.

"Oh my gosh," I thought. "That's the best-looking guy I've ever seen in my entire life."

As I walked by him I felt an electric rush—it was like the ding-ding-ding of a slot machine paying out. It was crazy. I went to the ladies' room, and on the way back when I tried to sneak a peek at him he was ready for me. He smiled and winked.

He waved me over and gestured to an empty stool next to his. I shook my head and motioned for him to come over to where I was sitting. But he turned away. So I shrugged and went back to my friends. I was certainly not going to dance to some strange guy's tune—especially if he was going to be cheesy and wink at me.

A little while later he walked over with another guy and they introduced themselves. His name was Trevor and the other guy was his brother Peter. They sat down at the table next to us. We started talking, and I immediately thought Trevor was very intense. He explained that he was a retired Navy SEAL—everything he did was intense.

I really didn't know anything about Navy SEALs. That just wasn't my world. So he started telling me all about his life. I was completely, thoroughly, utterly charmed. Trevor had been married once before, and he had a seventeen-year-old son who was already making noise about following in his dad's footsteps and becoming a Navy SEAL. He lived in Virginia Beach in an extended Navy community, and went back and forth to visit his parents in Hendersonville, Tennessee, where he'd grown up.

Trevor was very attractive, my favorite combination of muscles and machismo, and he ticked off some other important boxes for me. He'd served his country, traveled and seen the world, raised a child, cared enough to visit his family, and rode a Harley to boot.

We talked for several hours, and then it was time to go home. To make my intentions clear, I gave him my business card. With a dazzling smile, he immediately got the message.

I said, "If you're in town for a while, just give me a call. I find you pretty interesting—and you seem like a nice guy."

He called me the next day and suggested that we meet up somewhere later. I agreed, so he said he'd call me back within the hour with a plan, but he flaked out and didn't call back. I thought, "Okay, maybe he's not so interesting."

But he called me the next night and said, "Hey, we're downtown."

I said, "I'm in Brentwood. Do you want to come down here?"

He answered, "Well, we might come down." But he flaked out again.

I should have just dropped the whole thing right then and there.

The third day he called again. "Hey, I'm here with my brother. Do you want to—"

I cut him off. "No, thanks."

Trevor could hear the disdain in my voice. "Look," he said. "About last night—"

I cut him off even harder. "Do you know baseball?"

"Yeah," he said carefully. "I know baseball."

"Well, you know how foul balls count as strikes?"

"Yeah."

I lowered my voice. "Well, that's you. You've taken two big swings and hit two foul balls. Which means you've got two strikes on you. Three strikes and you're out, dude."

"What are you talking about?"

"You jerk me around one more time, and I'm done with you."

There was a pause as he thought this over. "Okay, message received."

So we started over again, and this time we really hit it off. I was curious about why he lived in Virginia Beach. He explained that there was a sizable Navy retiree community, he could stay in touch with his old SEAL brothers, and many of his best friends were still in the service. He was clearly still attached to his old life in a big way, and I didn't hear much about his plans for post-military life. Later I learned that most of these vets never really leave the military behind. And throughout coastal Virginia, Navy SEALs are like rock stars to the locals, kind of like in the movie *An Officer and a Gentleman*. Lots of townies look to marry Navy guys; they're called "frog hogs." But I had no idea what the significance of all this would be in the months and years to come. At that moment, I eagerly soaked it all up.

Trevor stayed in town for two weeks, and we went out and had a lot of fun. But I noticed a few odd things about him. For example, he *never* picked up a check. He liked to go Dutch, and in some cases he didn't even chip in at all, which really rubbed me the wrong way as a hardworking house cleaner who'd learned to stretch a dollar. Whenever the bill came, he acted as if we were just friends and he hadn't asked me out on a date. Normally I never would have tolerated this kind of behavior, but in every other way he seemed to be wooing me. When he went back to Virginia I didn't really know where I stood.

I became friends with his brother and offered to fix him up with some of my friends. He was a good guy, but whenever we talked about Trevor, a strange tone crept into his voice, as if he were suddenly talking to the cops. He'd say, "Gina, you seem like a nice girl. You know, my brother's never going to get married again."

But the problem was I'd fallen for Trevor, and hard. I realized for the first time in my life I finally knew what real, deep, aching, maddening, overwhelming love felt like. I suddenly wasn't interested in anybody or anything else. I blew off other guys who showed some interest in me, and even though I kept telling myself, "No, don't do this!" I couldn't help myself. I had to have Trevor. That was it.

My friends had met him, and they were decidedly underwhelmed.

"Why are you with this guy?" they asked. "He's too slick."

"He's got cold eyes . . . he gives me the creeps."

"I thought he was kind of a jerk."

"Gina, he doesn't have much personality."

"He's too intense."

"He's probably cheating on you with those frog hogs."

But I would not be deterred. "No, you're wrong. He's wonderful. He's a war hero."

Everybody tried to warn me, even his own brother. But I wouldn't listen.

All I knew was that Trevor made me feel safe, he was hand-some and manly, and, according to him anyway, as a trained and battle-tested Navy SEAL he could kill people with his bare hands. This guy was so intriguing—he was turning out to be my ultimate macho dream guy.

Eventually he came back to town after a few months, and we hung out again. He helped me clean houses, and we'd go to lunch. I was crazy about him, but he always kept me at bay. I'd try to hold his hand or kiss him but he'd gently demur; I reckoned he just wasn't ready for it. I was a little confused. If he was hanging out with me and going housecleaning and all that, wasn't he falling pretty hard, too?

But I didn't dwell on it. I was gone, over the moon.

- - - - - - - - - - -

Lessons for Life and Business

Always know what business you are getting into. Take the time to learn it from the ground up, and gather as much knowledge as possible to fully put your ideas into play. Build your business with your own hands, surround your creation with positive energy, and nourish and protect it every single day so it has a real chance to flourish.

SPICE-RUBBED BEEF TENDERLOIN
with MUSTARD CREAM SAUCE

*S*ometimes when I get tired of chicken and the "other white meat" won't do, I follow my purest carnivorous instincts and go right for the red meat.

I love serving beef dishes at the Sunday dinner parties I host for family and friends, and this is one of the more popular recipes!

Please feast freely on this dish—and don't be shy about mopping up extra sauce with Angel Biscuits (page 147). You won't regret it!

INGREDIENTS

SPICE-RUBBED TENDERLOIN

Vegetable cooking spray

2 1/2 tablespoons kosher salt

1 teaspoon black pepper

1 teaspoon dried thyme

1 teaspoon garlic powder

1/2 teaspoon ground cumin

1/2 teaspoon paprika

1/2 teaspoon ground red pepper

1 beef tenderloin (5 to 6 pounds), trimmed

2 tablespoons olive oil

Continued

SPICE-RUBBED TENDERLOIN

• Preheat the oven to 475°F. Grease a roasting pan with the cooking spray.

• In a small bowl, stir together the kosher salt, black pepper, thyme, garlic powder, cumin, paprika, and red pepper.

• Rub the tenderloin evenly with the olive oil.

• Sprinkle the salt mixture over the tenderloin, pressing to adhere.

• Cover with foil and let stand for 30 minutes at room temperature.

• Place the tenderloin in the prepared roasting pan.

• Insert a meat thermometer into the thickest part of the tenderloin.

MUSTARD CREAM SAUCE

1 tablespoon olive oil

$1/2$ onion, minced

1 garlic clove, minced

1 cup dry white wine

$1/4$ cup stone-ground mustard

2 teaspoons sugar

8 ounces low-fat sour cream

1 teaspoon kosher salt

$1/4$ teaspoon black pepper

- Bake at 475°F for 15 minutes.

- Reduce the oven temperature to 375°F and bake for 25 to 30 minutes, or until the meat thermometer registers 130°F.

- Remove from the oven and let stand 10 minutes before slicing.

MUSTARD CREAM SAUCE

- In a medium skillet, heat the olive oil. Add the onion and sauté for 2 minutes.

- Add the garlic and sauté for 1 minute.

- Stir in the wine, mustard, and sugar.

- Bring to a boil and cook, stirring constantly for 3 minutes, until thickened.

- Remove from the heat and whisk in the sour cream, salt, and pepper.

- Pour over the tenderloin and enjoy.

ANGEL BISCUITS

This is my go-to biscuit recipe.

I don't make many breakfasts during the week because life is so hectic. But there's always the weekend . . . we can sleep in and make a big breakfast: these fresh-baked biscuits with butter and blackberry jam along with some bacon, quiche, and a hot cup of tea—oh my goodness, I'm in heaven! It's so easy to gobble up three of them. Then I skip lunch and work out extra hard that day!

It's all a balance, right? :)

INGREDIENTS

2 cups all-purpose flour

1 1/2 tablespoons sugar

1 tablespoon baking powder

1/2 teaspoon salt

1/2 cup butter flavor Crisco (or just butter, if you prefer)

3/4 cup milk

- Heat the oven to 425°F. Grease a baking sheet pan.
- In a bowl, mix the flour, sugar, baking powder, and salt.
- Cut the Crisco into the flour mixture with a pastry cutter until fine crumbs form.
- Stir in the milk and blend until well combined.
- Turn the dough out onto a lightly floured surface.
- Knead lightly, then roll the dough out to about 1/2 inch thick.
- Cut with a biscuit cutter. (Yields 10 to 15 biscuits, depending on how big your biscuit cutter is.)
- Place the biscuits on the prepared baking pan. Make sure they are not touching.
- Bake for 9 to 10 minutes, until slightly brown on top.

BLEEDING PINK

- - - - - - - - - - - - - - - -

The Birth of Gigi's Cupcakes

*W*hile I was busy falling in love, something completely unexpected happened.

On Labor Day in 2007 my brother Steve called me from New York City. He was talking with his mouth full, and I could barely understand him.

"Gina, I'm standing in Central Park eating a red velvet cupcake," he mumbled. "You're not going to believe this, but I stood in line for two hours at this hotshot cupcake shop, Magnolia Bakery. This place is all over the papers; everybody wants one of these cupcakes. And they're like five bucks!"

I was cleaning a bathroom, and for some reason his cupcake review seemed ill-timed.

"You know, I'm happy for you that you're eating a five-dollar cupcake. But I got to go and clean a toilet right now."

"Wait!" he yelled. "Don't hang up! That's not why I called you."

"So why did you call me?"

"You and Mom make way better cupcakes than these guys. I don't think these are very good. I'm telling you right now I think you should open up a cupcake shop in Nashville. You'll make a fortune."

I looked in the bathroom mirror. I was wearing my pink rubber cleaning gloves, and I looked sweaty and tired.

"That's very interesting," I murmured.

Steve knew I had been experimenting with recipes for several years, baking cupcakes and cookies and breads in my home kitchen to give to my friends and family at Christmastime. And I'd always do my Hunka Chunka Banana Love in a bread loaf tin and wrap it up as a holiday thank-you gift for my clients. Everybody really liked my stuff, and the cupcakes were especially popular. I tested everything out on my friends and had begun assembling a portfolio of can't-miss recipes.

But could I actually turn it into a full-time business as Steve was suggesting?

"Gina, you bake stuff that's much better than this. Do me a favor. Just think about it."

I glanced down at the hair-clogged shower drain, a pile of dirty towels in the corner, and the nasty toilet I was about to scrub.

"Okay, I'll think about it."

And before I even hung up the wheels were turning.

Why not start a cupcake shop? It sounded like fun. I'd always been willing to try something new, to step out on faith. Maybe Steve was right. I could reinvent myself again if I wanted to. What did I have to lose? How hard could it be?

That night I sat down with a legal pad and wrote up the pros and cons. I started to grasp that it might be possible. I created a basic plan of how many cupcakes I'd have to sell, what kind of equipment I'd have to buy, how many people I'd need to help me. I'd have to get a business loan. But I had energy, a great track record, and most important, a bunch of great recipes.

My gut was screaming, "Just do this."

I talked to my mom and dad. They were all in on the idea. Ever the entrepreneur, my dad laughed and said, "Just go for it!" Even Trevor thought it sounded good, and Clement Pepe told me I had nothing to lose by trying.

As it happened, the next week I was booked on a quick trip to Mexico with my friend Ami Kerr and a couple of her buddies. We were only supposed to be gone for three days, but all that changed when a hurricane hit the Gulf of Mexico on our second day. (Note to self: Don't go to Mexico in September. It's cheaper because that's hurricane season.)

On our first day in Mexico I curled up in a cabana on the beach and read *Your Best Life Now* by Joel Osteen. His words about the power of positivity and applying your talents to better your lot in life struck a chord in me, especially as I thought more and more about Steve's cupcake shop idea.

On the second day the storm hit, and it got really scary really fast. The rain blew so hard that parts of the hotel roof came off. Our room flooded. Then the hotel staff came around passing out life vests and warning everyone that the nastiest part of the hurricane was about to hit. Soon patio chairs, umbrellas, and pieces of the hotel were flying around, crashing into windows. It was terrifying. The rain came down so hard it looked like a solid surface—you couldn't even see through the heavy curtains of water. Inside our room, water came in through the ceiling, under the windowsills, up through the floorboards. The balcony upon which we'd planned to sun ourselves was a disaster zone.

Ami and I rode out the hurricane together and decided the whole trip was a "character-building experience." After three tense days and multiple canceled flights, weather delays, and traffic jams, I finally got back to Nashville. I literally kissed the ground and cried. I was back in America, thank God.

I went home and sat back down with my legal pad and a rough business plan for my new venture. I was ready to pull the trigger. Now I was on a mission. If I could make it through a hurricane, I could handle a cupcake shop.

– – – – –

Historically speaking, the cupcake occupies an interesting space, and the patriot in me has always been intrigued by how it became such a staple of American desserts. Many of the sweets that we list on our national bill of fare can be traced back through the centuries to our origins in England and other European countries. Pastries, pies, cakes, biscuits, shortbreads, muffins, and tarts can be found in most Western cultures and are thus part of our culinary DNA. (Ah, if only the nations of the world would put the same amount of energy into getting along with one another as they do into devising elaborate desserts . . .)

So where did the cupcake come from?

From my reading and research, I discovered that from the founding of the Colony and Dominion of Virginia in 1607, right up until the last year of George Washington's second term as president 190 years later, every cookbook published and sold in the Thirteen Colonies was British. The British had no cupcakes, just traditional breadlike "tea cakes" and something called a "fairy cake"—which was smaller than a teacup, bigger than a biscuit, and crunchy like a cookie.

It wasn't until 1796 that Hudson Valley domestic kitchen laborer Amelia Simmons pulled her favorite recipes together and self-published the charming, handmade *American Cookery*, the first truly American cookbook. The thin volume gave readers a road map for creating dozens of dishes that had delighted the provincial palate for eight generations. It referenced ancestral favorites from England, Holland, and Scandinavia, but most notably it introduced such local American inventions as apple pie, scrapple, grits, pancakes, and cream cheese. It also marked the first appearance of recipes featuring indigenous— that is, Native American—ingredients such as maize ("Indian meal"), beans, pumpkins, rye, and squash.

Tucked into those forty-eight pages were the instructions for baking "a light cake in a small cup"—the first official reference to a "cup cake" in the Americas. Using butter, flour, sugar, and eggs, the cake described was sweet, soft, and moist, more like a layer cake than a hard British biscuit—a cute, small, single-serving treat that anybody could love.

By 1828 the term "cupcake" was in general use, and people created them in cups, tins, and ramekins, filling them with custard, whipped cream, butters, jams, and all kinds of fruits. For most of the next century the cupcake remained primarily a homemade product.

In 1919 Indianapolis baker Alexander Taggart introduced the Chocolate Cup Cake as the world's first mass-produced snack cake, and it was an instant success. The convenience it afforded was revolutionary. Instead of bothering with a messy slice of last night's dessert wrapped in wax paper and lugged around in a lunch bag, you could now dash into a corner shop and pick up a reasonably priced, nicely packaged portable treat that could fit in your pocket. The Taggart Baking Company sold its cupcakes at local grocers and in countless five-and-dimes, general stores, and candy stores, slowly moving them out across the Midwest.

When Taggart introduced its signature runaway-hit Wonder Bread in 1921, the company became a target for acquisition. In 1925 it was purchased by Continental, America's largest commercial bakery, also the home of the Hostess brand. In short order, alongside Wonder Bread and the Hostess Twinkie, the Hostess CupCake was rolled out internationally, and it became a global smash, a mass-market masterpiece. For the next hundred years it remained a favorite all over the world, and it established a baseline for commercial baked goods.

In 2016 Hostess sold more than 600 million CupCakes, proof that after a modest eighteenth-century launch and more than two hundred years of trial and error, the cupcake was an all-time favorite, a fixture, a staple—a truly American original.

– – – – –

I decided I wanted to create cupcakes like no one had ever seen or tasted. I wanted to infuse them with qualities that would prove irresistible. I wanted them to be little works of art, small-scale celebrations that would excite people and, in a way, make them feel as if they were part of something special. I wanted each cupcake to provide a few moments of happiness.

I was developing a mission statement of sorts: I wanted people to get more than just a delicious cupcake—I wanted them to have a real sensory experience. I wanted them to taste my orange cupcake recipe and be transported back in time to a summer day in their childhood, to relive the joy of peeling the wrapper off an orange push-pop from an ice cream truck. I didn't just want to fill their mouths with regular old lemon-flavored cake; I wanted to jolt their taste buds to life with the unmistakable, electric zing of freshly squeezed lemon juice. Chocolate that made them swoon, red velvet that melted on their tongues, strawberries that tasted like they had been picked that very morning—that was what I was after. I knew my recipes would make or break me, and I was confident I could compete on that level.

Everything else was a mystery that needed to be solved. What did the boutique cupcake business really look like? Who was out there—and what were they doing? Could I find a niche that I could call my own? What kind of cupcakery could I realistically create? More important, what would I have to do to get people to show up?

There were only a few real players out there, and they all had interesting origin stories. I read up on them with a mixture of admiration and envy, realizing that I wasn't the first person who'd dreamed this particular dream. But the more I studied, the more I realized there was an opening—there was always plenty of room for something unique.

My brother had visited Magnolia Bakery in New York's West Village, and it had really been the industry's major trailblazer. Its original founders, Jennifer Appel and Allysa Torey, are rightfully credited with starting the trend of gourmet cupcakes shortly after the shop opened in 1996. Magnolia was a traditional upscale bakery when Appel and Torey started using their leftover cake mix to create dazzling cupcakes. Their regular customers flipped, and word of mouth spread. Then the shop was featured on HBO's *Sex and the City*. It became everybody's favorite sweet spot and ignited the cupcake boom in New York City. Soon there were lines around the block and opportunities to expand. Appel and Torey sold their interests in the company in the mid-2000s, but Magnolia continued to prosper, eventually operating about twenty stores, including branches in the Middle East, Asia, and Central America. I really admired what they built and how they branded it.

Out west, Sprinkles opened its sleek, hipster flagship store in 2005 on Santa Monica Boulevard in Beverly Hills. Owner Candace Nelson's inventive use of sophisticated, high-end ingredients and her flair for nonstop innovation made Sprinkles an instant go-to destination for foodies and celebrities. Nelson broadened the Sprinkles brand to include cake mixes and ice cream—and even created an ATM that dispensed cupcakes! She became a celebrity herself, serving as a judge on the Food Network's hit show *Cupcake Wars*. Sprinkles eventually opened outposts in nearly two dozen other cities and built toward international expansion. That's what I call entrepreneurial excellence.

Among a few others I studied was Hey Cupcake! in Austin,

a popular regional operation that featured stores and a "cupcake truck"—a food truck outfitted for remote events. Hey Cupcake! was the first company to do "mobile cupcaking," an idea I instantly liked and made note of.

On the flip side of these success stories is a cautionary tale. Long before Gigi's Cupcakes launched, Manhattan-based Crumbs Bake Shop was the largest cupcake chain in the United States. Founded by Mia and Jason Bauer, the company went public on the NASDAQ and rapidly expanded to more than seventy locations in eight states. But over the years, the pace of events and a series of growing pains made it hard for the company to get into a groove and simultaneously fend off fierce competition. There was also internal pressure to change its business plan, and after unsuccessful efforts to expand its menu to restaurant-style food items and to introduce kitchen-oriented retail products, Crumbs filed for bankruptcy in 2014 and went completely out of business in 2016.

- - - - -

By the fall of 2007 I was ready to rock. I'd been thinking everything through and could see it, taste it, feel it. I talked with people I trusted—cleaning clients, friends in the business and banking worlds, people I knew who'd started their own companies. The majority of them—big-time success stories themselves—didn't quite get it. They were polite, but most tried to let me down gently.

"Well, you know you need a business plan . . ."

"You know you'll need a big chunk of money . . ."

"You'll have to find a way to secure investment capital . . ."

"You know location is everything—you have to find the right space . . ."

I could tell they were thinking, "God love her, poor thing, she has no clue."

Undeterred, I plowed ahead. This wasn't my first rodeo; I already knew what it was like to start a company that nobody else could understand.

I tentatively settled on a name for my new venture—"Gigi's Cupcakes," which I hoped sounded familiar and personal, and also subtly conveyed that each cupcake would be a handmade, home-style creation.

For many years now I had been wedded to my nickname "Gigi," which was used interchangeably among friends and family along with my given name "Gina." When I was a teenager, my brother Steve had a beautiful daughter right out of high school, and I babysat for him and his young wife all the time. The little girl's name was Allisha, and I loved my niece with all my heart. When she was a baby she couldn't say "Gina"— it always came out as "Gi Gi." Soon everyone was calling me Gigi, and it stuck. And I have been Gigi ever since.

I researched the name and filed for a trademark. Then, noodling around on the internet, I was thrilled to find that "GigisCupcakes.com" was available. My brother Randall happened to be in town, and he suggested I consider a more playful name. We spent the rest of the evening kicking ideas around but came up empty. And wouldn't you know it? When I went back online to buy the GigisCupcakes.com domain name— somebody else had snapped it up.

A little later I discovered that two girls in New Jersey had started a company called Gigi's Cupcakes. I owned the national trademark, but technically I couldn't stop them from calling their store Gigi's Cupcakes. So I settled for "GigisCupcakes USA.com" and decided not to worry about the New Jersey girls. After all, I thought I was going to have only one store; New Jersey wasn't going to hurt me.

— — — — —

Several months had gone by without much contact with Trevor, who, despite my new business adventure, was still very much on my mind. Secretly, I ached to see him again and was growing frustrated with the circumstances that were keeping us apart.

We'd talk on the phone and he'd tell me about his efforts to jump-start a second career. He was having a hard time finding something that was a good fit and seemed to be living mostly off his modest military pension, which explained a lot—for instance, why he wouldn't pick up checks and always insisted on going Dutch.

While I was brainstorming my new cupcake shop, Trevor came back to Nashville to see his family, and I allowed myself to get excited. We made plans to have dinner the night he arrived. But with no heads-up of any kind, he chose to meet with his family instead. It was several days before he even called. He offered no apology or explanation, and his tone seemed to imply I had no voice in the matter. He proposed another time to get together, but I passed. I was not happy about how he was treating me and I wanted to think about it. Despite my feelings

for him, my friends' and family's cautionary words were ringing in my ears.

My brother Randall couldn't believe what a jerk Trevor
was. "Gina, he's totally yanking you around. It's been what,
six months since you met him, and he's still acting like he's not
even sure he wants to see you. He won't pick up a check—he
won't even hold your hand. What's this guy's problem?"

I decided to confront it head-on. I met Trevor for dinner a
couple nights later and pressed him for an explanation for his
behavior.

He hemmed and hawed. "I don't know if we're ready for the
next step."

I called for the check.

"Listen, Trevor. I'm done being your buddy. I've got enough
buddies. For six months I've been waiting to see where this was
going, and it doesn't seem to be going anywhere good. Let me
be clear: I don't need a playmate and I don't need a boy toy.
I don't want to just date around and see who I get sentimental about at Christmas. I'm looking for something real. I'm all
grown up and I thought you were, too. But maybe I was wrong
about that."

I paid the bill—of course—and left.

Later that night he texted me, "Hey, do you want to do
something tomorrow with my cousin and my brother?"

I couldn't believe it.

I texted him back, "Please don't contact me anymore."

Well, in short order I discovered that Trevor didn't like
being told no. He took my brush-off as a challenge, and in true

gung ho SEAL team tradition he texted me fifteen times that night, each time sending me a question mark.

I didn't answer. Finally, right around midnight, he showed up unannounced at my house.

I opened the door and he stood there, shifting his weight from foot to foot, trying to gauge my mood.

I sighed. "Well?"

"I need to talk to you. Just give me ten minutes."

Now, of course I was still in love with him, and as much as I wanted to close the door on him, I just couldn't. He came in and started pacing around my living room.

"I think we're supposed to give this a try, I really do. I want more."

I was flabbergasted. "Really? Because you sure don't act like you want more. You treat me like I'm just somebody to go bar-hopping with. That doesn't work for me."

He stared at me frankly. "Does this work for you?"

And for the first time he took me in his arms and kissed me for real—and it was everything I'd hoped it would be. I felt like I'd known him forever.

Trevor stayed for the rest of the weekend. Suddenly we were in a relationship. We went out and listened to music, had dinner, laughed and carried on. I had a great time. The only rub happened when we decided to go to a Titans football game. I asked if he could cover his own ticket because they were $120 apiece. He said sure, but then balked when it was time to pony up. I held my ground and he wound up paying his own way. But he was not too happy about it.

After a few days he had to get back to Virginia Beach for a meeting with his realtor. He'd been trying to sell his property so he could move to Nashville to be closer to me. A few hours after he left, I was cleaning up the kitchen and happened to hear a text message alarm. Trevor had left his cell phone on the coffee table. On the screen was a text from someone named Linda. The text read: "Where are you? When are you coming home?"

My antennae went up. I was tempted to go through all his other text messages. But despite my conflicted feelings, I just didn't want to stop trusting people. Instead, I sent his brother Peter a text that read, "If you talk to Trevor tell him he left his phone at my house."

Somehow Peter got hold of Trevor, who drove all the way back from Chattanooga to get his phone. When he arrived, I asked who Linda was. I could see the wheels turning as he realized I'd seen something on his phone.

"She's just an ex-girlfriend."

I let it slide. "Okay."

There was a moment when he couldn't tell if he was in trouble or not, but finally he took the phone, gave me a kiss, and headed back out to his car.

Our emotional "commute" began in earnest. And I have to say, we mostly behaved like a real couple. He'd come to town and we'd go look at houses and daydream about the future. But he always held back a little, and I never could tell if it was out of financial need or emotional terror.

He'd say, "Well, it's a great house, maybe if you buy it . . ."

There was never a discussion about pooling our resources,

but I knew his military pension was not huge. My friends pointed out that he knew my cleaning business was purring along and he'd already demonstrated a tendency to freeload.

"Gina," they'd say, "you're running one business and starting a second. Don't pay his way—you can't afford it."

I decided to follow their advice—not just as a practical matter, but also as a test to see if and how he might step up. One night at dinner I slid the check over to him and said, "Your turn."

He blinked, not sure what was going on, then slowly reached for his wallet. "Are you okay?" he asked cautiously.

I smiled. "I'm fine."

He got the message. He was going to have to start paying his way in Gigi World.

– – – – –

Nashville in the mid-2000s was a progressive city with a sterling reputation for supporting all manner of small local businesses. There was huge money in the country music business, the medical and publishing industries were thriving, and there was an exciting culinary explosion in Music City.

Importantly, there were lots of foodies and new bars and restaurants all over town, which fueled my hopes that financial institutions would be supportive of my idea to do in Nashville what had worked so well in New York, Washington, Austin, and Los Angeles.

I'd been a Bank of America client for nearly twenty years, first in Southern California with my bands and my first house-cleaning business, and then in Nashville with my professional music career and my new, expanded, blue-chip Gigi's Cleaning Company. I had done all my personal and corporate banking with B of A and had mortgages, loans, and credit cards with them. And through it all, a great guy named Terry Porter had been my banker, taking care of all my needs.

So naturally, I went to Terry to get some operating capital for my brand-new cupcake business.

"Terry," I began, "I'd like to get a business loan. I'm going to open a cupcake shop."

He narrowed his eyes, as if he were trying to decipher a foreign language. "I'm sorry, darlin', what did you say? Cupcake shop?"

"I'm going to open a cupcake shop."

He waved his hand at me. "Can you shut the door for me?"

I got up, shut the door, and sat back down.

He smiled kindly. "Best if we discuss this in private. So you want to do a cupcake shop."

"That's right. Just like Magnolia in New York City and Sprinkles in Beverly Hills. Except my recipes are better."

He wrinkled up his nose at me. "Are you crazy?"

"I don't think so. I think I can make money at it. Here's my business plan."

I handed him a spreadsheet I'd worked up that showed my start-up costs, operating costs, and a breakdown of how many cupcakes I'd have to sell at what price over what period of time to turn a profit. It was simple, I admit, not a particularly fancy presentation. But the numbers were solid.

He read it over, looking up at me occasionally as if somebody might burst in and tell him he was on *Candid Camera*. He put the spreadsheet down and picked up his phone. "Hey, Peter. Can you come in here real quick?"

I started to ask, "What do you—"

He held up a hand. Peter, another guy I'd worked with at the bank over the years, came in. He recognized me at once. "Hey, Gigi, what's going on? You doing good?"

"I'm doing real good."

"How's business?"

"I'm starting a new company."

Peter smiled big. "That's terrific, congratulations! Another cleaning company?"

Terry waved him quiet. "Listen to this."

"I'd like to open a cupcake shop."

They looked at each other, then back at me, then back at each other. Suddenly they both doubled over with laughter.

"Are you kidding?" Peter said.

"Um, no, I'm not kidding. What's so funny?"

Terry shook his head and tried to break it to me gently. "Honey, we can't give you a loan for a cupcake shop."

"Why not? I've been in business for eighteen years. I've got excellent credit. I've got a little savings. All my bills are paid off. I've got a home. I'm a successful businesswoman. And there are people making lots of money in other cities with this very same idea."

Terry patiently responded. "Well, it's just too risky. What if you went to all this trouble and nobody bought your cupcakes?"

"I don't get it. You loan a million dollars to a hillbilly singer to buy a tour bus that depreciates thirty percent the minute he drives it off the lot, a guy who may not sell a single record or a single concert ticket. But a longtime customer like me can't get a hundred grand for a concept that is already a proven winner?"

Peter was classy but firm. "I'm really sorry, Gigi."

"Okay. Just remember I came to you first."

Terry held out his hand. "And I do appreciate your loyalty. Sorry we couldn't help you with this."

I went out and sat in my car. "Wow," I thought. "They were actually laughing at me. Did that just happen?" But I would soon find that they weren't the only ones who thought I was out of my mind. I went to four more banks, and they all laughed in my face.

I went home, shocked. After a couple of days went by I had an idea. I realized there was more than one way to skin this cat. I called Terry back. "Hey, Terry. Can I come and see you again?"

He moaned. "Uh, Gigi, I don't have time . . ."

"Just five minutes."

I went back in and said, "You're not giving me a regular loan, and no one else will. But you're a nice guy, I know—even though you laughed right in my face."

He squirmed. "Gigi, I didn't mean to insult you—"

"No worries," I said, cutting him off. "But there is a way you can help me out with this. I've got a line of credit with you and a bunch of credit cards. I want to take out advances against all of them." I spread the cards out on his desk.

He said, "Well, that's pretty risky."

"Okay, then give me the loan. But I know I have a thirty-thousand-dollar line of credit here, and it's all secured. I want the money."

He thought about it, then finally said, "Well, okay. But the interest rates could kill you."

"I'm not going to have the money out for long. Don't worry about that."

So I got my first $30,000 from Bank of America.

Then I called Capital One. "I'd like to take out an advance for thirty thousand dollars, please."

The guy said, "Ma'am, your total line is thirty thousand dollars."

"I know, I'd like it all. And since I've been such a great customer, I'd be grateful if you could do better than the twenty-two percent interest rate—can you do fifteen percent?"

The Capitol One guy balked. "Well, we can't just change the interest rate like that."

"Sure you can! If you don't, then I'll have to go somewhere else. You can see I've got excellent credit. Come on, isn't there any way you could do it for fifteen percent?"

I heard some keys clicking, then he sighed. "Okay. Thirty thousand dollars at fifteen percent."

I'd been in business with American Express a long time, and I had American Express OPEN for Small Business. I called them next. "You know, I've been with you a long time and I need a loan." They gave me $15,000 at 9.5 percent.

And then on to Discover Card. "I need a small business loan." They offered me $32,000 at 18 percent, but I haggled with them for two days, finally talked to the right person, and got it down to 11 percent.

I rounded up all this money and put it in the bank.

$107,000.

Now it was time to find the perfect spot.

－ － － －

The Bristol on Broadway was a relatively new high-end condo-
minium complex in a great area between downtown and Music
Row that catered mostly to young, upscale clients—lots of
bachelors, businesspeople, doctors. I got my foot in the door at
the Bristol cleaning two nights a week before the building even
opened, keeping the terrazzo and the public spaces gleaming as
well as keeping up the furnished demo condo units. I would see
lots of big shots, industry types, and rich yuppies going in and
out of there. Most of them looked down their noses at li'l ol' me
with my buckets and mops and cleaning truck. But I didn't care;
I was there to make money.

Eventually I started cleaning for about a dozen Bristol residents. One of them became one of my all-time favorite clients:
Neil Clark, a great, creative guy who was positive about everything. He always wanted to hear how things were going, what I
was up to, and what I had up my sleeve.

Neil happened to be home one day while I was cleaning his
place, and I told him the whole plan of my new cupcake business. He was excited and promised to let me know if he came up
with any great ideas for me.

The next day he called me.

"Honey, I know you're going to do this cupcake shop and
I love you and I'm going to support you. I forgot to tell you
there's a little place for lease right across the street. I can see

it out of my apartment window. It's a fabulous location. You should come down and meet me right now and take a look."

My brother Randall was staying with me while he job-hunted, so we jumped in the car and headed downtown. I hoped Neil's suggestion was as good as it sounded, because the Broadway area was just starting to get hot but hadn't exploded yet. It could be a great spot for my new business.

It was about six o'clock on a Sunday in late September, and it was getting dark. Neil was waiting for us. I recognized the building; it was the old Steak-Out restaurant, which had a sit-down area and a take-out area. According to the For Lease sign out front, the sit-down area, about 999 square feet, was being subleased by the restaurant, which would continue to operate its take-out business in the back. Evidently the owners realized they could make $4,500 a month just by having someone rent the front half of the building.

I peered through the window. The place had been cleared out, and it was a wreck. Dirty floors, holes in the walls, broken fixtures. But I could see the potential. I could envision myself baking in there; I saw customers coming in. I must have had a weird expression on my face because Neil was looking at me funny.

"Are you okay?" he said.

I smiled. "I'm getting the chills. This is it."

And Randall said, "No, no, no. You've got to look around, check out some other places."

I shook my head. "No, this is it." It was the strangest thing. It was like I was fast-forwarding a movie to the part where I was already open and operating the world's greatest cupcake shop. I could see it.

Neil said, "Don't you want to shop around a little?"

"Nope. This is it."

The For Lease sign said, "Call Alan Thompson." I called him right then and there and left him a message.

The next morning Alan Thompson called me back. And my life changed forever.

− − − − −

"Well, hi, Alan. This is Gina, Gigi Butler."

He asked, "Which is it—Gina or Gigi?"

"Well, it's both. I go by both names, either one's fine."

"Okay," he said patiently, as if everyone had two names.

"Alan, I'd love to lease your space. Can I meet you today and get a tour of the place?"

His voice was measured. "Do you have any experience in retail? The reason I ask is that I already have a letter of intent from another party who wants to put a bar in there."

"Oh, no, don't put a bar in there. I don't see a bar there."

He sounded surprised. "Sorry? What do you mean you don't see a bar there?"

"Can you just meet with me?"

He agreed, and we set a meeting for later in the day at the Broadway Brewhouse, a joint in the neighborhood where we could comfortably have a conversation. I got all spiffed up, put my best pantsuit on, did up my hair and makeup, and drove downtown with my little business plan.

We sat down in the bar area, and with no preamble Alan asked, "So what would you like to put here?"

"A cupcake shop."

He winced. "A cupcake shop? Do you know how high the rent is? It's forty-five hundred a month. That's a lot of cupcakes."

"I'll make it work."

He was very polite, but his voice was firm. "No way. That'll never work."

"I can do it. Here's my business plan. Just look it over."

He flipped through my few pages, thinking it over.

"I'll call you after I take a look at it. But no promises."

To be fair, my plan wasn't very sophisticated. No smoke and mirrors. But it was simple to digest, nice and clear. Start-up capital was $70,000. An industrial fridge was $5,000, a used bakery oven about $10,000. Mixers, pans, bowls, tools, another $10,000. Insurance, sinks, furniture, signage, employees, supplies, etc., another $45,000. I estimated a 78 percent gross profit on each cupcake sold, not including labor.

I didn't hear anything from Alan the next day. I called him before the close of business but he didn't take my call. The next day I called him three times and left a voice message. "Alan, please meet with me again. I really want to do this . . ."

He finally called me back. "Okay. I'll meet you, but it's not going to work. I already signed an LOI. We're gonna put a bar in the building."

So we met in the parking lot.

I said, "You know what, Alan? God has given me this vision that I'm supposed to do this. I don't know why, but I'm certain I've been called to do this."

Alan rolled his eyes. "Oh, so now I'm going to piss off God if I don't do this deal with you?"

"Well, basically . . . yes."

He laughed. "You are feisty, aren't you?"

"You read my business plan. All I have to do is sell two hundred and fifty cupcakes a day."

"You're dreaming. You won't even sell fifty."

I kept at it. "You shouldn't put another bar here. You need something to pretty up this corner. You don't need an old bar here."

"Bars make money."

And right at that moment, as if by divine design, a guy came out of the Broadway Brewhouse, stomped on a cigarette, and threw a beer bottle against the brick wall.

I grabbed his arm. "Is that what you want on this property? You don't want that mess."

Alan looked at me funny, as if I'd set the whole thing up.

"Look, I feel kind of sorry for you. I know you want this, and maybe you can make it work. But it's not the kind of deal I like to get involved with."

I got serious. "Please. At least just think about it."

"Okay. But I've already signed the LOI, and when the money comes through, that's it."

I didn't leave him alone. I called him ten times a day. I'd say, "Let me take you to lunch. I have a better business plan. I've tweaked it."

He finally grew exasperated. "This isn't just my property. I have partners. Homey Aminmadani and Farzin Ferdowsi own it with me. They came from Iran forty years ago and opened a Taco Bell. Now they own hundreds of franchises. These are serious guys. I can't ask them to fool around with a little cupcake shop."

As luck would have it, the daughter of my dear friend Jenny Collins was best friends with Homey's daughter in school. I asked Jenny if she'd help get me a meeting with Homey.

So Jenny called him and told him how great I was and what a hard worker I'd been, a nobody who'd come from nowhere to build a successful small business. She must have done a good job selling me, because Homey asked Alan about me.

Alan admitted, "Gigi's very persistent. Maybe we should give her a chance."

And Homey said, "Do you think she could sell any cupcakes?"

Alan shrugged. "Who knows? But if anyone in the world can do it, it's Gigi. I've never met anyone like her. She's got all this energy and she just won't give up."

Now, Homey was a really good man. He might have been a tough businessman like Alan said, but he was open-minded and curious. He agreed to meet me.

I got my spiel all ready. I wore all pink, and I took a dozen of my best cupcakes. I didn't even wait for him to start telling me how tough retail could be and what he was worried about.

"Homey, someone gave you a chance when you arrived here. Isn't that why you came to America? To find a better life? To make your dream come true? All I'm asking is that you give my dream a chance."

He stared at me. I wasn't sure, but I was wondering if he might just throw me out of his office. Then he sighed and nodded slowly. "Well, Jenny called me, and she said you're a wonderful girl."

"I am. Let me prove it to you."

"What you want to do is very expensive."

I pulled out my cupcakes. He powered a couple of them down and licked his fingers.

"Well?"

He regarded me evenly. "Okay, this is a pretty good cupcake you have here. You put up three months' rent and you can have it. Thirteen thousand five hundred dollars."

I almost fainted with joy. "Thank you, Homey."

"Don't let me down."

I asked, "What about build-out?"

He shook his head. "No way I'm giving you build-out money. You take the property and build it out any way you want. You get three months for twelve thousand. That's it. Take it or leave it."

A serious guy, indeed.

I shook his hand and got out of that office before he had a chance to change his mind.

— — — —

The problem was that I didn't have three months' rent on hand. I had already mapped out how I would spend all my credit card money on equipment, a contractor, and furnishings. I looked at several scenarios, but ultimately my mom and dad came to my rescue and loaned me enough to cover the first three months' rent.

I finally signed the lease in November. The twelve grand covered December, January, and February. I was going to have to start paying rent on March first. Which meant I had about ninety days to design, build, outfit, staff, open, and begin operating Gigi's Cupcakes.

Dale Denny, my old church buddy lawyer who'd graciously handled my divorce, was not optimistic. "Look for someplace else, Gigi. This rent is too high. I've looked this contract over. They're not giving you build-out money; they're not doing anything to help you succeed. It's all on your shoulders."

"I know, but I have to be at that location. I can just feel it."

He sighed. "You're liable for five years' rent at fifty-four thousand dollars a year—that's two hundred seventy thousand dollars, an awful lot of money. If the shop doesn't take off, you'll go broke. And the landlords will take everything you own."

I heard his words, but my gut still screamed, "Yes, yes, yes—go for it!"

He shook his head. "Okay, but as your attorney, I'm advising you not to do this."

I was calm and confident. "Trust me. That corner's going to come alive and stay hot for years to come. I know it. I'll be fine."

I don't think he believed me. But the die was cast.

All I had to do now was . . . well, everything.

- - - - - - - - - - -

Lessons for Life and Business

Knowledge is power, so make sure you know more about your business than anyone else. If you don't know what you're doing, people around you may perceive you as weak and take advantage of you in ways you'll never see coming. Learn everything you can so you can maintain the upper hand.

GNOCCHI MAC AND CHEESE

*T*here are lots of steps to this, but it is SO worth it!

I don't make this very often, but when I do it's a crowd favorite. I served this at a Gigi's employee party once, and two years later they still ask for it. It is memorable, to say the least. You can also lower the fat and calories by using low-fat cheese. It's just as tasty.

INGREDIENTS

Vegetable cooking spray

2 tablespoons plus 1 tablespoon kosher salt

Two (16-ounce) packages potato gnocchi

3 tablespoons butter

3 small green onions, finely chopped

3 tablespoons all-purpose flour

1 teaspoon fresh thyme, finely chopped

2 tablespoons fresh rosemary, finely chopped

2 1/2 cups low-fat milk

2 tablespoons Dijon mustard

1/4 teaspoon hot sauce

4 ounces sharp cheddar cheese, grated

4 ounces extra sharp white cheddar cheese, grated

1/4 teaspoon garlic salt

1/4 teaspoon black pepper

- Preheat the oven to 375°F. Grease an 11 x 7-inch or 2-quart baking dish with the cooking spray.

- In a large stockpot, bring 3 quarts water with 2 tablespoons salt to a boil.

- Add the gnocchi and boil until the gnocchi floats, about 5 minutes. Drain.

- In a large nonstick saucepan, melt the butter over medium heat.

- Add the onions and sauté until soft, about 30 seconds.

- Add the flour, thyme, and rosemary.

- Cook for 3 minutes, stirring constantly, until golden brown and smooth.

- Gradually whisk in the milk and increase the heat to high.

- Bring the mixture to a boil, reduce the heat, and simmer, whisking constantly, for 5 minutes until slightly thickened.

- Stir in the mustard and hot sauce. Remove from the heat.

- Add the cheeses and stir until melted.

- Stir in the gnocchi and the 1 tablespoon kosher salt, the garlic salt, and pepper.

- Transfer to the prepared baking dish.

- Bake for 25 minutes, or until the gnocchi is puffed and the sauce is golden and bubbly.

- Turn on the broiler and broil for 2 minutes, until the top is slightly browned.

- Let stand for 5 minutes before serving.

GROWING PAINS

- - - - - - - - - - - - - -

Gigi's Cupcakes Arrives

I started building out the first Gigi's Cupcakes shop in November. My parents, celebrating Mom's cancer remission and excited by my new project, came in from Texas and generously pitched in on the next phase, which was right up their alley—Dad liked to build things and Mom was a whiz in the kitchen. And I was happy to have some comrades in arms.

We dove right in, tackling the ramshackle space and all its flaws. My dad had to grind the floor to make it flat so we could install nonskid tile, and he worked with a cabinetmaker to get my cases and counters constructed. Between housecleaning appointments I'd zip by the store, and he'd have a bunch of samples ready for me. I'd select colors and textures and he'd dutifully go off to round up Formica trays, glassware, and plumbing fixtures.

I went bargain hunting in Nolensville and found a used industrial three-hole sink that fit my small kitchen space. But the guy wanted too much for it. When I told my dad about it, he shook his head. As a seasoned entrepreneur, he understood the value of jumping on a bargain when you found one. He said, "Go back and get it today."

"It's seven hundred fifty dollars, Dad."

"If you piddle around you're still going to have to find a sink, but it's going to cost twice as much at the last minute."

He was right, of course. When I went back to buy the sink, the guy loaded it in the truck for me.

"You're starting a bakery?" he asked. "I've also got some pans for sale."

I perked up at this. "I'm looking for flat pans."

"Yup. Got a whole bunch. I'll sell 'em all for two hundred dollars."

"Make it one fifty and you got a deal."

Turned out he was also selling some café tables. Perfect. I grabbed them, too.

I haunted all the restaurant supply stores in town and hit a bunch of garage sales. I met a guy who had a bakery in Hermitage. He sold me his mixer, an old Hobart model, one of the best mixers in the world.

I wasn't interested in doing a normal-size cupcake, so I needed a big-size cupcake pan. Online I found a pan that could accommodate a bigger liner so I could bake a larger cupcake.

I picked up some high bar stools at Costco. Then I cut a deal with one of my cleaning clients: I traded him a free month of maid service for a sandstone path outside the store.

I had a great electrician named Jimmy Rice who came in and

taught me everything I didn't know about electricity. I showed him where I wanted everything placed, but I didn't understand I had to have different connections for some of my industrial appliances. For example, he told me it would cost extra to wire up a huge oven.

My dad called him up. "Hey, Jimmy, can you just help us out? Can she just give you some cupcakes for the plug and throw in a hundred bucks?" So Jimmy did the plug on the cheap.

Parking got worked out with Alan, but I had to fight to get complete control of the spaces on my side of the building. I got little signs made up that read: "Be sweet—please only park here 15 minutes."

As the build-out neared completion, everything seemed to be purring along. Although I hadn't yet settled on which brands of my biggest items to buy—ovens and fridges and mixers—I had a plan. I'd also started to finalize my recipes and menu, and was working out staff needs, a logo, and some graphic elements.

We had a couple of ugly surprises. First, we had a plumbing issue. Our water heater wouldn't pass inspection, and appointments to get equipment approved had to be made weeks in advance. But we hustled, found a replacement, and had it installed just minutes before the inspector showed up.

Then a biggie hit us broadside. In December my dad called me while I was working at a cleaning job. "You're not going to be able to open."

"Why is that, Dad?"

"The government control guy came by and said you have to

put a fifty-gallon grease trap out by the street. It's going to cost a ton."

And that's how I learned that every restaurant has to have a fifty-gallon trap, a stand-alone filter that goes underneath a restaurant's main sink and catches all the grease produced in an industrial kitchen, diverts it from the sewer system, and keeps it from getting into the city's water supply.

Personally, I didn't see the rationale. Gigi's Cupcakes wouldn't be a restaurant. I wouldn't even be using a fryer. I wouldn't produce any waste grease at all. I could see why a grease trap would be needed for a place that was frying food all day and producing huge amounts of grease. But I wouldn't be doing any of that.

I did a little research and found that a fifty-gallon trap would cost $35,000. It seemed to me we should be able to get by with a *five*-gallon grease trap instead—a $5,000 item. I knew a fifty-gallon grease trap was overkill. So why did the city and county insist on it? Was it a kickback thing? Or a laziness thing? I needed to get to the bottom of this.

My dad was way ahead of me. "I already got you a meeting set up with the county inspector. Tomorrow at noon."

So I got all dressed up the next morning, packed up my best cupcakes, and went downtown to see the government dude. Now, by this point I'd already stood in line many times at the county clerk's office waiting for permits and paperwork, so I was fully prepared to jump through a hoop or two.

I was ushered into the inspector's office. I whispered a silent prayer. "God, please help me to find favor with this man. Please, a little miracle would help."

The guy's name was Charlie, and for a bureaucrat he was

okay. But he didn't seem too inclined to accept my arguments about the grease trap.

"Let me save you some time," Charlie began. "You have an oven so you're going to have to have a hood, correct?"

"Yes."

"And you use butter and lard and oils in your recipes?"

"Well . . . yes. But not in amounts that would require a fifty-gallon grease—"

He cut me off. "So that's a yes?"

Hmmm . . . this guy was a pro. There was only one thing for me to do. I decided to take command of this meeting. I couldn't just sit there and let him run his little playbook on me—"One plus one equals three, so buy the $35,000 grease trap or else."

I smiled sweetly and said, "Thank you for taking the meeting with me. First of all, I'd love for you to just experience these cupcakes before you say anything. Just please experience it."

Suddenly he was on unfamiliar ground. "I don't have a fork and . . ."

"Oh, I have one." And I set a little picnic basket on his desk—with a little pink plate and a plastic fork and a napkin. "Just try one before you say no."

"I'm not saying no. You just need a fifty-gallon—"

Now I cut him off. "Charlie, can you please just try this?"

He looked into the box and eyeballed the different cupcakes I'd brought. "Which one should I have?"

"Do you like chocolate? Vanilla? Are you a strawberry person?"

"I'll take a strawberry."

I served one up. "Here's a strawberry. And do try the red velvet."

"I can't eat two."

"Just a taste before we talk business. It's important you know what we're talking about here—which is *cupcakes*."

So he starts eating. "Wow. This tastes like my great-grandmother made it."

"That's because it's *my* great-grandmother's recipe."

And I told him the history of my family recipes.

"Charlie, you don't know my background. I clean toilets for a living, and I don't have thirty-five thousand dollars to spend on a grease trap, especially one that I don't need to bake cupcakes."

"Well, that's not my problem."

"I don't think it's fair that I should have to spend thirty-five thousand dollars on something that we both know I don't need."

"The regulations—"

"C'mon, Charlie . . . have a heart, just have a heart."

Through his mouthful of red velvet cake he sputtered, "Miss Butler, you can't just come in here and guilt me."

"Look, I'm not frying anything. I'm baking it . . . with love. Love and passion. It's the American dream, Charlie—that's what you're eating right now, the American dream."

The last of the red velvet disappeared into his mouth. "That's a pretty amazing cupcake."

"Please let me get a five-gallon grease trap. It's only five thousand dollars. I can afford that. I won't dump grease into the city water supply, I promise. Please, just put a stamp right here. Please. That's all I need."

He didn't say anything for a minute. "I need a couple days to think about it."

So close. But I didn't have a choice. It was up to him now.

"Okay, but please let me know as soon as possible. Don't let my American dream disappear down a fifty-gallon grease trap, Charlie!"

He laughed. "You are so dramatic. Were you in the arts?"

"I was a singer."

"Of course you were. Go on, get out of here. But leave the cupcakes."

The next day he called me back in.

"After my wife ate your cupcakes and guilted me up one side and down the other about helping a small businesswoman get started, I really had no choice. Give me the paper. I'm going to pass you."

Another bullet dodged.

— — — — —

I hadn't settled on an approach to packaging yet, and I needed a logo. I'd always assumed I'd think of something clever, clean, and artistic, something that reflected the purity of my mission and the uniqueness of my approach. Problem was, I was drowning in details and minutiae, and I hadn't yet come up with anything.

I hired a graphic design guy to rough out some packaging ideas, but he came up empty. So I went online and bought some simple, classy items. White boxes with separators, simple bags, functional labels, and tissue. No award-winning designs— yet—but certainly nicer stuff than you generally saw. I'd order stuff every month, single boxes, six-boxes, four-boxes. I was winging everything, just winging it.

My dad didn't like it. "That's too expensive. Just use plastic clamshells."

"I'm not doing plastic, Dad. That's not what bakeries do. That's what Kroger does."

I sketched out my first logo on a bar napkin at the Tavern restaurant with my friend Jenny Collins. Since the frosting swirl was going to be the signature feature of my cupcakes, I played with several versions before settling on the basic pink corkscrew design used today. I handed it off to a friend who knew a little about computer graphics and, poof, we had our first working logo.

There were so many other things to think about. Where do people sit when they come in? What do my napkins look like? Should I build a stand-up bar to keep things moving, or should I encourage people to sit down, get comfortable, and hang out?

I knew I wanted soccer moms coming in to buy dozens of cupcakes at a time, so I decided to build the shop for speed, more like the Baskin-Robbins model than the Starbucks model. I'd have just enough minimal comfort for my guests to sit for a few minutes, eat something, and then be on their way. Although I loved Starbucks, I didn't want Gigi's to be a place where people hung out all day and only spent a few bucks.

My schedule was getting pretty crazy. I'd literally work from four in the morning until I'd drop, usually around midnight. For the first part of the day I'd clean houses, and then I'd dive into the build-out of the store. It was crazy, but I needed the cash flow so I had no choice.

We got the floors in, painted the walls, and pulled the kitchen together: prep tables, shelving, mixers. My mom tracked down the mixing bowls I wanted and helped me organize spatulas, spoons, spreaders, and icing kits with dispensers and tips.

I had an idea for shirts my employees could wear that were emblazoned with mottoes and sayings like "Live life one cupcake at a time!" and "Everything's sweeter with Gigi's." I couldn't afford to get them right at the beginning, but I made a note to buy some as soon as I could.

I could afford a little plastic sign with my first logo, and I put that up. I mounted my new company's address over the door—1816 Broadway, Suite A. They were just stick-on letters and numerals from Home Depot, nothing fancy—but I felt as if I were planting a flag on a mountaintop. Today, they're fading and peeling, but I don't have the heart to replace the originals—they've become sentimental reminders of where my journey started, and I really like seeing them every time I go into the shop.

Gigi's Cupcakes was almost real now, taking shape moving closer and closer to opening day. As October and November gave way to December, I could see my plan was finally, at long last, coming together.

– – – – –

Though I'd baked cupcakes for my cleaning business clients, family, and friends, I'd never produced more than twelve dozen at a time, and I got all my ingredients at the retail level. The logistics of managing supplies, buying in bulk, and rationing material loomed as a challenge. How many eggs and how much sugar and flour would I need every day? Where was the best place to buy stuff? It was time to get serious, and there was only one person who could help.

I called Aunt Bennie and told her, "I'm going to open up a cupcake shop."

She was thrilled. "Good for you!"

"Can I come and hang out for a week or so? I need to pick your brain about all this."

"How soon can you get here?"

Aunt Bennie ran a classy, full-on bakery called The Cakery in Southlake, Texas. Bennie was a genius of sorts, famous for her huge, elaborate wedding cakes, as well as her breads and cookies. Her bakery was a special place—the kind of place that mattered, that played an important role in its community, always a part of weddings, graduations, bar mitzvahs, celebrations, birthdays, and yes, funerals and farewell parties. She never advertised and was content that word of mouth would do the trick. And she was right.

So Mom and I went to Texas for boot camp at The Cakery. Bennie knew what I was up against, and she was unfailingly encouraging. She wanted to help me prepare, and confided that she'd been ready to share all her secrets with me for some time.

Our mission would be to perfectly orchestrate a subtle blend of elements that would result in, well . . . the perfect cupcake.

Bennie began by reminding us that people "eat with their eyes," and that the first step to enjoying a dish is being taken in by it visually, when the snapshot in your brain triggers your salivary glands. While I was at The Cakery I often waited on people who came in to order or pick up things, and I noticed how much pleasure they took in the visual impact of Bennie's creations. She was right.

Bennie said, "Remember, things have to be beautiful."

We worked our way through such subjects as recipes, ingredients, materials, and equipment. Bennie said, "Baking is a series of chemical reactions, made by people with the right know-how and the right tools and ingredients. That's why everything from a bakery tastes different." Sometimes her lessons were about the order in which you do things—add baking soda at the end, fold butter in after you've baked the crust, and so on. Sometimes the sessions were about various "secret ingredients" that were only available commercially, and that would help me develop and refine my signature recipes and frostings. Sometimes they were about finding new uses for old ingredients, or new ways of using old techniques.

So I would try to master the "base" of a tuxedo cake or a chocolate cake, getting the proportions just right and adding enough elements to make them singular, different from ordinary batters. Going this extra mile would make my cupcakes special. It was exciting, and my mom and I got swept up in the experimentation, working long days that actually felt like they blew by.

After about two weeks, we went home and I was ready to refine my recipe list. I decided to perfect about twenty-three different recipes for Gigi's Cupcakes, and I thought I could lock them down at the rate of about five or six per day. So I spent a solid week making each recipe and tweaking it until it was perfect.

My first menu covered a lot of ground.

Gigi's First Cupcakes

COCONUT: White cake with fresh coconut milk buttercream frosting and shaved coconut.

LEMON DREAM SUPREME: Yellow cake with lemon filling and lemon buttercream frosting.

TIGER TAILS: Yellow cake with raspberry filling and fresh coconut.

BOSTON CREME: Yellow cake with vanilla creme filling and chocolate ganache frosting.

TEXAS MILK CHOCOLATE: Milk chocolate cake with chocolate frosting and a yellow fondant star.

MIDNIGHT MAGIC: Devil's food cake with chocolate buttercream frosting and mini chocolate chips on top.

WHITE MIDNIGHT MAGIC: Devil's food cake with cream cheese frosting and mini chocolate chips on top.

CHOCOLATE RASPBERRY: Devil's food cake with raspberry filling and raspberry buttercream frosting.

ROCKY ROAD: Chocolate cake with chocolate frosting, nuts, and marshmallows.

SCARLETT'S RED VELVET: Red velvet cake with cream cheese frosting and one white chocolate heart.

STRAWBERRY SHORTCAKE: Fresh strawberry cake with strawberry buttercream frosting.

GINGERBREAD: Gingerbread cake with cream cheese frosting and a homemade gingerbread cookie boy on top.

KIDDIE CUPCAKE: White cake with blue buttercream frosting and a gummy worm on top.

BIRTHDAY SURPRISE: White cake with fluffy pink frosting and sprinkles.

TIRAMISU: Yellow cake with coffee/Kahlúa filling, cream cheese frosting, and chocolate powder.

PUMPKIN SPICE: Pumpkin cake with cream cheese frosting and one candy pumpkin on top.

CARROT CAKE: Carrot cake with cream cheese frosting and a candy carrot on top.

APPLE SPICE: Apple cake with raisins and nuts and seasonal streusel topping.

BLUEBERRIES AND CREAM: White cake with blueberry filling and frosting.

CHOCOLATE MALT: Yellow cake with malt, marshmallows, chocolate malt frosting, and a malt ball on top.

HUNKA CHUNKA BANANA LOVE: Banana bread cake with pecans and chocolate chips.

PEANUT BUTTER CUPCAKE: Milk chocolate cake with peanut butter cups baked in and peanut butter buttercream frosting.

TOP HATS: Devil's food cake with buttercream frosting dipped in chocolate ganache.

Before I left Texas I had showed Aunt Bennie something I'd been working on for a while—the "Gigi swirl," a grand, swooping crown of frosting that I intended to make the signature element of every Gigi's cupcake. The swirl wasn't just frosting on top of the cake; it was a statement of both quality and delicious decadence, and it had to be just right. Make it too sweet, and people wouldn't be able to finish it. Make it too tall, and it might fall over. Make it too light, and it wouldn't taste like a one-of-a-kind dessert. I knew that the swirl could make or break my new enterprise.

Bennie was impressed. "This is perfect," she said. "This is how you put your own stamp on the cupcake, and make it different from all the other cupcakes out there."

I needed to perfect the swirl so the frosting would stay high and tight. I wasn't sure I had the right mix of ingredients, especially to mass-produce hundreds of cupcakes every day.

Bennie instantly grasped what I was talking about. She knew that frosting was the key to the success or failure of any type of cake. Assuming the body of the cake itself is flavorful, moist, and gently sweet, frosting can either spur the creation to its fullest, richest potential—or ruin it with cloying granularity or waxy blandness. A good cake with perfect frosting will never leave a slimy film on the inside of one's mouth.

I started playing with different ingredients to find the right balance of flavor, texture, and strength. What if I added butter and vanilla and milk? Whole milk? Nonfat milk? Each had different properties. I thought the nonfat yielded the best flavor, so I went with it. And then one day, bang—there it was, the perfect swirl with the perfect properties. I brought everybody in to taste it, and the verdict was unanimous. It had a homemade flavor, and it just might have been the best frosting anyone had ever tasted. I was over the moon—I'd finally nailed down the recipe for what would become both the signature and anchor of Gigi's Cupcakes: a nice tall frosting that holds it shape, is not too sweet, is creamy, and fills up your mouth in a luxurious way.

Bennie and my mom were experts at pulling together elements from across the culinary spectrum and applying them to their recipes. I was amazed at how much variety they could get from just a handful of staple ingredients. They reminded me that every element in a cake comes from somewhere else and is usually made by someone else—sugar, spices, flours, fruits, nuts, chocolate. The genius of a great baker is knowing how to seek out those building blocks and fit them together so that they all harmonize in a perfect recipe. It was an important lesson, and it opened my eyes to new possibilities.

After I played around with this idea for a while, I realized the same principle could be used to create many more recipes. For instance, I took fresh strawberries, powdered sugar, butter, vanilla, and milk—and that became my signature strawberry frosting. If I added cream cheese, caramel, or peanut butter to my basic buttercream, I'd get a whole other recipe. With Bennie I learned that the possibilities for creating intriguing flavors and textures were endless—I would be limited only by my imagination.

– – – – –

While I was perfecting my recipes, the contractor was getting close to finishing, and we needed to outfit our kitchen. It was time to gather the few remaining tools of the trade.

Bennie said, "You've got to get yourself a Doyon oven—it's

the best oven in the world. Restaurant suppliers will try to get you to buy a bread oven, but trust me, you want a Doyon. It's the Mercedes of ovens."

And like a Mercedes, a Doyon ain't cheap. I called the factory and said, "I'd like a Doyon bakery oven, please. How much will the basic model cost?"

"For just one oven?"

"Yes, please. I'm opening up a small bakery."

"Thirty-two thousand."

After I'd caught my breath, I asked how much of a discount I could get.

"No discount."

"Okay, I get it," I said, accepting the inevitable. "I'll take one."

I'd done my homework and I wasn't going to quibble. The Doyon is a double oven that bakes twenty-six dozen cupcakes in twenty-two minutes. You can run one oven up on top at 375°F and you can run the other at 315°F, a handy feature because my different cake recipes bake at different temperatures. For example, my lemon Sprite cake bakes at 325°F, but my Texas milk chocolate cake bakes at 350°F, and the white cakes bake at 315°F. I need an oven that can multitask. And this thing is right on temperature every single time. Worth every penny when you consider how many cupcakes a busy Gigi's store has to produce daily.

With this kind of precision, you can refine your baking schedule and pinpoint your inventory needs. From mixing the batter to putting a finished cupcake on the shelf is only about an hour. It's not uncommon to have twenty dozen freshly baked cupcakes ready to go when we open our doors at 7:00 a.m. We have to maintain that kind of output if we hope to simultaneously sell cupcakes at a retail location and also meet the needs of our catering clients and people who like to pick up several dozen each day for their workplace.

The morning I left to go back to Nashville and prepare for the opening, Bennie and I had a cup of tea. I thanked her for all the help she'd given me and all the wisdom she'd shared. I wasn't sure how I could ever repay her.

"Repay me?" She laughed. "You've already repaid me. You're carrying on the family tradition. You're making sure our recipes never die."

I could feel tears coming to my eyes. I'd taken my place in the line of family bakers and I was about to carry everything forward for another generation.

Then Bennie mentioned something that I'd never considered before. "You have to have a food purveyor, you know."

"What's that?"

"You're going to go through a huge amount of groceries every week. You've got to buy in bulk and stock your shelves without breaking the bank. You can't buy all this stuff at Kroger. You have to get on a food truck route."

All that made perfect sense to me.

So when I got home I started looking for a food purveyor.

I called PFG.

They laughed. "No, you're too small."

I called Sysco.

"A cupcake shop? No, we don't have time. We're busy."

I called US Foods.

A new guy named Bryan Flume was on the beat at US Foods. "A cupcake shop?"

"Yes. I need butter, and your McCormick vanilla in a gallon, and powdered sugar."

I ran down my entire menu with him.

"Well, that's pretty ambitious. Maybe you should start smaller."

"No, everyone's telling me to just use cake mix with no chocolate chips. But I'm going to do a homemade cake and put little Ghirardelli dark chocolate barista chips in it, and I'm going to fold them in there so there are little bursts of flavor in every bite."

"It's going to be more expensive," he warned.

"Yes, it will, but I want to have my own shtick. If I've learned anything from all my years onstage and being around stars and big-time businesspeople, it's that you have to have a shtick. My cupcakes have to be original, not like cupcakes you can get at Publix. It has to be something different or people are not going to come."

Bryan was sold. "Okay, I'm in. We'll get you set up."

"I'll be a good customer, you'll see!"

Bryan was a good guy. He helped me in lots of ways, not least of which was taking mercy on me and delivering goods at the last minute and adjusting my orders as I taught myself how to order supplies in bulk. He rooted me on as I built the business. He'd always tease me whenever he saw my name or a mention of the shop in the newspaper, and he'd bring his other customers in to see my strange little handmade operation at work. I could tell he took a kind of quiet pride in having helped me get started.

An old colleague of Aunt Bennie's named Curtis also wound up delivering supplies to me from time to time, and he was another cheerleader who lent me a hand whenever he could. Curtis and I worked together for a couple of years and then we lost touch.

Recently I went to Austin to speak at a General Mills convention, and Curtis was there.

"Remember me? I was there at the beginning of Gigi's."

"Of course I remember you!" And I hugged his neck.

Now Curtis is a big regional guy at General Mills. I was glad to see one of the good guys win for once.

Although I'd learned a lot about business, recipes, leases, permits, and lots of other stuff, one of the biggest skills to perfect was getting the balance right with the food purveyor. For instance, I didn't know how much powdered sugar to order.

Bryan would ask, "Well, how many cupcakes are you going to sell?"

"I don't know yet."

"Well, how about we start you off with six fifty-pound bags and see what happens?"

So I'd get six bags of fifty pounds each, and the next week I'd know if that was too much or too little. Today Gigi's buys about 2.1 million pounds of powdered sugar a year, so I eventually got the balance right—and I hope all the food purveyors who'd laughed at me in the beginning now take me seriously!

– – – – –

The oven and the refrigerators and the food deliveries were set up. We had a store that was about ready to open. We had pots and pans and spatulas and spoons. We had a logo and some cupcake boxes. We just needed a few more warm bodies.

I eyeballed a handful of people I thought we might be able to hire. My first employees included a bright college kid named Leah Parker, a middle-aged woman everyone called Miss Sharon who'd cleaned my friend Jenny's house, and a guy named David who didn't last very long. As our little team hurtled toward opening day, things were going smoothly, and I was secretly hoping we'd gotten over the hump.

February 21, 2008, finally arrived, and Gigi's Cupcakes threw open its doors. As we've seen, that first day was a magical preview of what was to come. My team showed up ready to work; we baked a dozen different recipes, welcomed a curious group of customers, and sold 253 cupcakes—253 more than anybody thought we'd sell. I covered my costs for the day and even had a little left over.

I remember feeling exhausted and exhilarated at the same time. We'd done it; we'd gotten off the launchpad. Now all we had to do was build a following and sell a few more cupcakes every day from there on out.

We locked up and turned the lights off. I took the day's meager proceeds home and put them in a little cash box. I thought, "My gosh, I did this. This actually happened. I made this money here, all because of a crazy little dream." There was more than $200 profit on gross sales of just under $1,000! But could I grow to the point at which I could break even and keep the doors open? How was I going to do that every single week while I was still spending a good chunk of each day cleaning houses? But when I crawled into bed I didn't toss and turn. I knew we'd made a very good start.

The next day even more people came in, and we sold 310

cupcakes. We knew we were on the right path. Maintaining a good rhythm—and bringing in more customers—would determine whether or not we'd ultimately be a success. It was up to us . . . and to the cupcake-buying public . . . and to God.

At the end of the first week, I had enough money in my little cash box to cover rent ($4,500), pay my employees ($1,000), and take care of the week's food bill ($1,200). US Foods had taken me on as a client, but I was on "probation"; they wanted to see if I'd survive, so they made me zero out my balance every week. It was the price of admission, and I was happy to pay it.

I'll tell you, it felt good to sit down to write out all the checks by hand. After I'd paid everything, I had $332 left over. A wave of relief washed over me—I was running the business I'd dreamt of, the cupcakes were getting raves, and we'd broken even in our very first week! But I still had to pay the drywall bill, my credit card cash advances, and my parents' loan. Sure, it was a burden, but I thought, "Wow, this thing looks like it might just work."

The next week we cleared a little bit more profit, and the week after that even more. I saved up like a squirrel, dutifully filling up my cash box every week.

Although our food purveyor arrangement was working well for staple baking ingredients, as we rolled along we were learning about the limitations of our toolkit—we needed more pans, bowls, and spatulas. We went bargain hunting, gathered what we needed, and did our best to tweak everything so the store would operate at greater efficiency. The learning curve was not exactly steep, but it was ever-present.

I was always looking out for new problems and refused to dwell on our initial success. I got pretty critical about everything and was always trying to fix something, even if that thing wasn't broken. I was overwhelmed, burning the candle at both ends with the shop and the cleaning business. There was no time to sit back and enjoy any of it.

I finally realized I needed more help.

I'd had my eye on a down-to-earth, no-nonsense woman named Stephanie Babbs, who managed the Steak-Out next door and had been one of Alan Thompson's employees for sixteen years. Everybody called her "Babbs," and I'd gotten to know her while we were building out the shop. I'd swing by the Steak-Out occasionally and ask Babbs if I could use her bathroom, or I'd drop in and buy an iced tea. As I was refining my menu I'd test new cupcake flavors out on her.

One day Babbs came over and told me she'd like a part-time job with me. I'd watched her at the Steak-Out, and I already knew she was one of the hardest workers I'd ever seen. Plus, she had good, solid food service experience, and she knew both the building and the neighborhood, all of which I liked.

Still, I had to ask: "Don't you already have a full-time job?"

"Yeah, but I really want to be a part of this."

She told me Alan was very supportive of the idea and thought a change might do her some good.

"Okay, then," I said. "I could sure use the help. I'm still tied up cleaning houses. If you can help me smooth out some of the wrinkles here at Gigi's, you're hired."

So Babbs came on board part-time, and we started putting policies into place and making lists of things that we were going to do. She was a lifesaver. In between handling housecleaning gigs and juggling chores at the shop, I worked with her to put together a bake plan to do a better job of getting the store ready every morning. It was a big and important development, and Babbs quickly became a key player at Gigi's Cupcakes. If I was cleaning during the day I could rest easy knowing that she was covering for me and chipping away at my to-do list. Within two months Babbs was ready to move up and manage the place full-time, at which point we got Alan's blessing to make her a full-time employee.

One day shortly after we opened, Miss Sharon was sitting out front. She said, "Come meet my brother, Johnny."

I said, "Hey, Johnny. Nice to meet you," and I went inside to check on the store.

Miss Sharon followed me in. "Johnny's looking for a job. He wants to bake."

That was good enough for me.

"Tell him to be here tomorrow at five a.m. I'll train him."

He came in the next morning and, voilà, we had a full-time baker.

So now I had Miss Sharon, Leah, Johnny, and Babbs. And we were turning into a tight little team just as things were starting to get busy.

– – – – –

Each day the total number of customers would increase slightly, and our sales figures steadily inched up. Some days a line formed, and people would patiently wait for us to open. One day there was a lady waiting in line who bought six cupcakes.

She made small talk at the counter with me and seemed genuinely fascinated by the whole idea of the shop. I didn't know who she was, but apparently that night she went home and told her husband all about it.

Her husband turned out to be Terry Bulger, a news reporter for WKRN Channel 2, Nashville's ABC affiliate. The next day he called me and gushed about the quality of the cupcakes. He was a bit of a foodie, too, and wanted to share my culinary Cinderella story with his viewers. Since I had a marketing, advertising, and promotion budget of zero dollars, I readily agreed.

Terry and his crew came in a few days later and shot a great little piece, profiling me and showing off our picturesque new store right in the heart of the happening Broadway district. Terry closed the segment by urging everyone to come down and taste these phenomenal, one-of-a-kind cupcakes. I couldn't have written the script better myself! And sure enough, in the days that followed we noticed our foot traffic picked up about 25 percent. Some of the new customers mentioned they'd seen me on Channel 2 and were curious. The lesson was not lost on anybody. We needed to do more marketing.

Meanwhile, I was killing myself. Five days a week, I was up in the predawn hours, opening the store by myself around 4:30 each morning and getting the baking under way. I'd get everything ready and frosted, then I'd zoom off to clean houses from 9:30 until 2:00. I'd run home and walk Prancer, then drop him off at my friend Melanie's house near Belmont, where he'd hang out with her dogs for the rest of the day. I'd change clothes, wolf down a late lunch, then head back to the store and work until closing each night around 7:00.

I was baking between three hundred and five hundred cup-cakes each morning, and then Johnny would bake the rest of the day. Eventually he took over the early shift so I didn't have to be the first one in every morning and the last one out. He would bake everything, then Leah and Miss Sharon would come in and frost, and then Miss Sharon would clean the store from top to bottom. I finally found a couple of closers, some girls from Belmont University who wanted a job. Having them there took some of the heat off me in the afternoons.

But I was wearing thin.

— — — — —

About this time Nashville had started to become a hot vacation destination, so people from all over the country would wander in. I don't know how word was spreading, but it was.

A couple dropped in one day looking for the owner. I came out from the back covered in flour and icing. There was a long line snaking out the door, literally dozens of people waiting to buy cupcakes.

I was a little distracted. "Can I help you?"

The man introduced himself and said, "I'd like to open one of these cupcake shops in Indianapolis."

I blinked, not comprehending. "I'm sorry?"

He said, "I want one of these in Indianapolis."

I was confused. "A cupcake?"

"No. A store. I want to open a store."

"What are you talking about? I only have this one store."

He realized I was a newbie. "I'd like to franchise a store. I'd like to work with you to open a Gigi's Cupcakes in Indiana."

I still didn't get it. "What are you talking about?"

He gave me his card and asked me to think about it. He said he was in and out of Nashville a couple of times a month and would call in a couple of weeks. I pocketed the card and promptly forgot all about it. I had way too much on my plate to be worrying about selling cupcakes in Indiana.

Logistics and finances were becoming my hot-potato issues. I was constantly telling myself to be patient—there was a learning curve and some growing pains to endure, and it was still early days. But as we gathered momentum, it was becoming obvious that I needed to streamline the operational aspects of the company. Although we weren't making zillions of dollars, I'd never handled as much money as we were pulling in. I would go home on Friday night with $5,000 in cash and would manually count it out, thinking, "This is crazy." I didn't have a plan for managing profits. I would just plow everything right back into the business because it seemed we always had to pay off a bill here or there. I didn't really know what I was doing; I couldn't foresee where all this was headed financially. The nuts and bolts worried me endlessly. I knew I needed to get more sophisticated about handling payroll, paychecks, withholding, and so forth.

This was the first brick-and-mortar business I had run, and it felt completely different from the cleaning company, a totally new animal that I had to figure out. This was more than just me and my mops and pails. I now had a building and a product and a public to worry about.

Usually all my cleaning workers were freelance, so I would just give them a 1099 at the end of the year and that was that.

But it was becoming clear I couldn't do that with my employees at Gigi's Cupcakes.

One day Angela, a customer who was also a CPA, asked, "Do you need accounting services?"

With evident relief I said, "I sure do."

"What are you doing with your cash?"

"Well, I'm just taking it home and depositing it."

She clucked. "Oh, you have to make daily deposits."

Of course, I didn't know that most retail businesses made daily cash deposits at a bank. I didn't even know I needed a bookkeeper. I'd always handled the checks and bills for the cleaning company, so I figured I'd just keep doing it for Gigi's Cupcakes. I just thought I'd keep the cash and deposit it when I needed to write checks. It never occurred to me that the government would prefer a clear system.

So I hired Angela to straighten me out and get an accounting rhythm in place. We started doing daily deposits, and we got more sophisticated with our in-house financial operations.

I'd done one thing right. I'd opened the store with Micros, a computer-based cash register system—$5,000 very well spent. The system was similar to what you'd see in a restaurant, a computerized register with preprogrammed pricing and codes for everything so you could run credit cards; track sales and inventory; and generate hourly, daily, and weekly statistics.

- - - - -

Finding good employees was not easy, I was learning. Even though we'd engineered a basic balance for keeping Gigi's Cupcakes in operation, we were always on the lookout for new talent, somebody who could come in and help with the crushing daily load.

Early one morning after we'd been open a few months, I was out sweeping the parking lot, getting ready to open the store, when a little old lady walked up to me.

She announced, "You're the cupcake lady. I need a job."

Knowing that my team and I were absolutely thrashed, over-worked, and overtired, I was receptive. "What can you do?"

"Just clean. That's all. But I work hard."

I looked her over. She was a wiry African American matron, seventy-five years old or thereabouts, no more than a hundred pounds soaking wet. But she looked tough and she had a deter-mined gleam in her eye.

I nodded. "Okay, we could use a good cleaner."

I told her what I'd pay her and what I needed her to do. She nodded agreement at each point and then gave me both barrels. "I'll clean whatever you got and work as hard as you need. But I don't want to talk to anybody. And don't you ever let anyone touch me. I don't want to be touched."

"Fair enough," I said, and took her inside.

"Everyone, this is Miss Martha, who'll be cleaning the store every day starting right now. She does not want to be touched; she does not want to be talked to. Just let her do her thing."

And man, she'd get in there and clean. She was like a machine. The store was spick-and-span clean.

Once she sat down and said, "I need a break, Miss Gigi."

"Great, let me get you something to eat."

"Nope. I don't want a handout."

I gestured to a prep table where some takeout was piled up for the staff. "I got lunch for everyone today."

She shook her head. "I don't need other people's food. Did you not hear me?" She went and fished a packed lunch out of her bag.

One day one of the college girls made a mistake and put a hand on her shoulder in greeting. "How you doin', Miss Martha?"

Miss Martha freaked. "Don't you ever touch me!" she barked, and roughly pushed the girl away.

It suddenly occurred to me that I hadn't checked Miss Martha out at all, and that maybe she'd escaped from—or belonged in—a home somewhere. Or maybe she had been abused, or suffered from some form of PTSD. Whatever it was, it was weird.

The girl was understanding. "I'm so sorry, Miss Martha," she said.

But Martha pushed her again, this time up against the wall. Now the girl was getting a little spooked. I could see a red splotch on the girl's arm and immediately thought, "Lawsuit!"

Martha was fired up and dangerous-looking now. "She touched me. I told you don't ever touch me . . ."

I said, "Now, now, she didn't mean to touch you, Miss Martha. Calm down."

Mercifully, the girl was very understanding and didn't make a fuss. Her arm had a light scratch and that was about it.

But everybody gave Miss Martha a wide berth after that. She cleaned the store for two years, and then she came in one day and sat down.

"I need to retire. I'm just too tired now."

So she retired and went home.

A few weeks after she left I took some food over to her house. I was working up a little speech about how much we missed her when she opened the door. With no sign of familiarity or interest, she looked me up and down and spied the picnic basket I'd brought.

She curled her lip and muttered, "I don't want your food." And she closed the door in my face.

I stood there, unsure of what I should do. I knocked again.

"Miss Martha, if you don't want me to come in, that's perfectly fine. But please let me leave you this food."

There was a long pause before she answered.

"You can just leave it there on the porch."

Mission accomplished. As I turned to leave, I heard her voice one last time.

"Thank you, Miss Gigi."

Learning how to work with people was part of the job. I think we all learned how to not be mean, not treat people badly, not make people cry. Learning how to be gentle and make people feel good is a real skill—especially when a customer's yelling and being obnoxious. We ran into challenges every week when Nashville's more unfortunate souls would wander in. If we didn't give them a cupcake they'd start yelling and cussing, and with a line of people waiting to be served it became critical that we all knew how to defuse the situation, keep a nice bright smile, and make sure everyone walked away more or less happy. This philosophy flew in the face of most of my fight-or-flight instincts, but it remains one of the most useful concepts I've ever adopted.

- - - - -

As our first year wound down, we hit some encouraging milestones. Business was good for our first couple months; then it just took off and we grew like crazy. We wound up grossing $900,000. I'd been grossing $70,000 a year cleaning houses, which was pretty good, but this was something else entirely. I'd never dreamed of generating that kind of money in my life. All in cupcakes, no less!

The media had noticed us. Gigi's Cupcakes became a friendly Cinderella story for viewers and readers. Magazine articles, newspaper profiles, and radio and TV blurbs piled up. The award-winning TV show *Tennessee Crossroads* did a segment on me and my cupcakes, and the piece was so popular that some years later it would be ranked number sixteen among their top fifty all-time fan-favorite episodes.

I had found God's favor. It was a moment in time when everything lined up for me. I don't think I'd ever been more grateful for anything in my whole life.

In the middle of all this, Alan Thompson walked into the store.

He eyed me evenly and said, "I think I've got an idea about how we can take Gigi's Cupcakes to the next level. Would you like to discuss it?"

I was all ears.

- - - - - - - - - - -

Lessons for Life and Business

When your fears and insecurities take hold, don't back down. Don't let ill winds blow you off course. Stand strong and be brave. Brave people make things happen in this world, and courage begets respect.

GIGI'S CHICKEN POTPIE
with GIGI'S PIECRUST

*Y*ou can't get more Southern than this. The first time I created this recipe was for the TV crew of *Undercover Boss*. They had just flown in from Los Angeles, and I wanted them to experience a homemade Southern meal the night before we started filming. I was nervous and didn't know what adventure I was about to embark on and how life-changing it would be. They didn't know what to expect either. My friend Brad Harlan helped me make it special for them. This home-cooked meal really put everyone at ease. It amazes me how breaking bread with people can make new friends and bring lives together.

INGREDIENTS

CHICKEN POTPIE

1/2 cup butter

2 medium leeks, sliced

One (4.5-ounce) can sliced mushrooms

1/2 cup all-purpose flour

One (32-ounce) carton chicken broth

4 cups chopped cooked chicken

1 1/2 cups frozen peas

1 1/2 cups carrots, finely chopped

1/3 cup fresh Italian parsley, chopped

CHICKEN POTPIE

• Preheat the oven to 375°F.

• Melt the butter in a large skillet over medium heat.

• Add the leeks and mushrooms and sauté for about 3 minutes, until leeks are softened.

• Sprinkle with the flour and cook for 3 minutes, stirring constantly.

• Whisk in the broth and bring to a boil, whisking constantly.

• Remove from the heat. Stir in the chicken, peas, carrots, parsley, salt, and pepper.

• Make the piecrust (recipe opposite).

• Divide the piecrust dough into two balls.

$^1/_2$ teaspoon salt

$^1/_2$ teaspoon black pepper

1 large egg

GIGI'S PIECRUST

4 cups all-purpose flour

1$^1/_3$ cups (heaping) butter flavor Crisco

$^1/_3$ teaspoon salt

- Place each ball on a pastry towel and roll out into a $^1/_4$-inch-thick rectangle.

- Place one piecrust in the bottom of a 9 x 13-inch baking dish and poke with a fork all over.

- Add the filling to the piecrust.

- Cut the remaining pie dough into strips and weave on top of the filling in a lattice design.

- In a small bowl, whisk together the egg and 1 tablespoon water.

- Brush the egg wash over the pie.

- Bake on the lower oven rack for 30 minutes.

- Move to the top rack and bake for 30 minutes more, or until golden brown.

- Let stand 15 minutes, then serve.

GIGI'S PIECRUST

- In a large bowl, combine the flour, Crisco, and salt.

- Using a pastry cutter, mix until pea-size balls form.

- Add 12 tablespoons ice-cold water and mix until the dough forms a large ball.

- Split the ball into two halves. Use one half for the bottom crust and one half for the top.

EMPIRE

- - - - - - - - - - - - - -

Gigi's Cupcakes Takes Flight

$\mathcal{S}$oon after the original Gigi's opened, Alan Thompson took some of my cupcakes to a church event. He watched, amazed, as people gobbled them up, going on and on about how good they were. A light bulb went on above Alan's head, and he immediately saw the potential for something big.

Alan was a successful businessman who'd launched Steak-Out franchises and restaurant real estate deals, and he'd been thinking about selling cupcakes in a new way. He knew I'd established a fervent following, first with a few regulars on Music Row whom I'd baked for informally, then with the rank-and-file public who were putting my first store on the map. He thought I could grow my boutique shop in Nashville into a national chain that would sell gourmet cupcakes inspired by homegrown recipes. He wanted to set up a franchising operation, and he was convinced it could be a winner.

A few days after the church event he made his pitch. I had only one question: "What's a franchise?"

He laughed. "It's pretty straightforward. You've got a hot idea here, and if you move quickly, you can establish outlets all over the country. Normally, you'd build out a series of corporate-owned stores and retain ownership of them all, but you don't have the money to do all that right now. So the other alternative is to lease the rights to your concept to entrepreneurs who are willing to build their own Gigi's Cupcakes store. They pay a fee to get in, you supply them with what they need to run the business, and you collect a percentage of everything they earn under the Gigi's banner. This is basically how all food franchises work—McDonald's, KFC, Dunkin' Donuts, you name it. They own the store, but you own the concept."

This sounded interesting, but I was still trying to figure out how to clean houses every morning while my rookie team baked cupcakes down on Broadway. I had a hard time wrapping my head around the idea.

But Alan knew what I was thinking and tried to reassure me.

"Look, franchising is something I know inside and out. I can help you spread Gigi's across the country. We'll put together some financial partners who'll bankroll the expansion of the company, we'll pick up some steam, make some noise, and soon you'll have people coming from all over wanting to buy in. You've already been approached by some people who love your products and see the potential."

"Alan, I'm still paying off my start-up debt and I've got to stay current on all my bills. There's no way I can pay you to start a whole new division of the company."

"You don't have to pay me. You can give me a percentage of the company and I'll work for free for now. I'll make money on the back end, once we're up and running."

He already had a list of what we needed to do.

"We need a big chunk of money to do this right," he said. "That's to get a couple more stores going, start some serious marketing and imaging, and get the ground softened up for a franchising effort."

Alan had lots of contacts throughout the food service and financial communities, and he thought over the next few months he could reach out to many of them to help us get rolling.

I thought about Alan's proposal for a few days. I got some books and started reading about franchising. Hmm. I thought Alan might be right—this could be a very good thing.

I went back to him with a slightly different take on it. I had been working two jobs, paying off the drywall bill and my loans. And I had managed to save $26,000, not through brilliant financial planning, but because I was just working so hard that I didn't have time to spend money on anything.

"I think instead of bringing in investors and giving up ownership, let's take my twenty-six thousand dollars and use it to start a franchise company. Will that be enough?"

In this scenario, we'd do it on a shoestring budget. He and I would be partners in a small, low-overhead franchising company, and I'd bring my dad on board to help build out the first couple stores. I could get a small loan to help with equipment, and Alan would handle all the business—projections, contracts, financial documents, vetting potential investors, etc.

Alan thought it was worth a shot, so we decided to move forward. We settled on an eight-year agreement. I agreed to give him 20 percent of the company, plus 5 percent of the gross sales annually. Neither of us could foresee that we would get to more than a hundred stores off that initial $26,000 investment.

I had a real estate lawyer read the contract Alan drew up, which turned out to be a big mistake. It never occurred to me that I should have sought out an attorney with lots of experience in the franchise world.

My lawyer said, "Well, it's a pretty good contract. I think it will be okay."

But my dad didn't like it and warned me, "It's your company; you need to keep as much as you can."

I didn't listen. And much later, once we got rolling, it became clear that Alan was making more money off my business than I was. I eventually got a good lawyer and started probing for a way to claw back some of what I'd given away, which was odd, because while my lawyer was talking to his lawyer, Alan and I were working closely on franchising and expanding the company. We'd go on the road together and talk about the situation during long car rides. I'd say, "Alan, you're taking too much money."

"Well, you agreed to it. You signed the contract."

"Come on. I signed it, but I didn't know what I was doing."

He'd shrug and smile awkwardly. "Well, that's not really my fault, is it?"

In the end, Alan did restructure his contract. Another business lesson learned.

\- \- \- \- \-

To begin our expansion, I decided to do a second privately owned store—a store that I would finance myself and use for training. I found one in Cool Springs, about twenty miles south of the original store. I knew that I didn't have enough money to bankroll all the corporate stores we envisioned, but it was a start. I knew the company's lack of operating capital would ulti-mately prevent it from growing at a brisk pace and getting the Gigi's Cupcakes name out there, but I had to start somewhere, and I decided not to give away anything up front.

One day my landlords Farzin and Homey came in. They'd been watching, too, and they wanted to buy a piece of the busi-ness. They had good radar and could sense that Gigi's was about to get hot. But I politely declined.

They didn't like that answer. "You have no money; you have no business experience. We've been franchising for years. We've made a fortune. We can tell you what to do and how to grow this business."

I told them I already had a plan and thanked them for the offer.

I could see Alan was right—people with money *were* get-ting curious about Gigi's. It was as if they, too, knew we were pioneering something new: the first franchised cupcake shop in the world.

\- \- \- \- \-

When my first store opened in 2008, the recession was just hit-ting. I've often been asked how we survived and thrived in such a hostile economic environment. I have a theory, but it's not something that's been endorsed by any major economists or anything.

It seemed to me that when the downturn hit, people were scared so they pulled their money out of the market and laid low. Some were concerned about big companies and government, some wanted more control over their investments, and some decided to "invest in happiness"—in other words, they chose to put their money where they could see some tangible good being done. Many of these people saw that Gigi's offered its own little brand of joy, and they liked that. Soon nurses, pharmaceutical reps, doctors, businesspeople, dentists—a diverse and eclectic bunch—were lining up to buy franchises.

During a recession cash is tight, and everybody's looking for a bargain. So it seemed to me that expensive steak houses like Ruth's Chris or Stoney River must have seen their numbers drop, while mid-priced chains like Chili's or Applebee's probably saw theirs go up. And I guessed that investors probably began steering clear of "premium" restaurant opportunities at the same time, too. In this context, Gigi's would seem to be a bargain both to investors and to customers out for a night on the town. For instance, after a nice, affordable meal at a chain restaurant, instead of ordering ordinary desserts off the menu, a couple might drop into Gigi's for a cupcake instead—which was guaranteed to be of far higher quality than a mass-produced dessert at a chain restaurant, and at $3.25 a pop, a much better deal than a prepackaged slice of pecan pie for eight bucks. Everybody learned—and loved—that Gigi's offered the best, freshest, tastiest product, period.

Our customers were also intrigued by my Cinderella story—the maid who worked hard but overcame all the odds to make her dreams come true. We all love a good rags-to-riches story, and we all eagerly follow the exploits of passionate people because we want to see what will happen next.

I think this is part of what drew people to us in an otherwise troubled time. As we expanded, we saw the effect of it everywhere we went—loving Gigi's Cupcakes seemed to be an almost universal state of mind!

- - - - -

Part of our growth process involved perfecting the menu. It took a little while, but I started to understand what people wanted, what they liked and didn't like, what days they were more likely to drop in and buy something, and what times of the year would be slow.

I regularly sold out completely in the early months, so figuring out how many cupcakes to bake each day became the most immediate and important challenge. For instance, one day we baked a bunch of cupcakes and no one came. Like, nobody. At the end of the day there were four hundred cupcakes sitting on the shelves. I was mortified. I liked to keep the shelves full of fresh, colorful product, but I didn't want to go out of business because I couldn't crack a math problem. I thought, "How can we avoid doing this again?" And the experience posed a key question I'd never even thought of: What do I do with leftovers?

The object, of course, was not to have any leftovers at all. But I knew it would be impossible to know exactly how many

we'd sell. So I decided that, at the end of the day, rather than
throwing leftovers out or taking them home and eating them,
I'd box them up and take them to a homeless shelter, the fire
department, the cops, the rescue mission, or the children's hospital downtown. We started donating whatever was left every
day to some worthy group. Everyone got in the habit of taking
a box and dropping it off somewhere on the way home.

In that first year, we started a "bake plan," which helped us
decode the rhythms, ebbs, and flows of the business. Each week
we looked at the previous week and studied which flavors sold
the most, what was the most requested cupcake, the quantity
sold of each type, etc. Then we'd look at the upcoming week.
Was there a holiday? Was some big concert or ball game going
on? Was it spring break? The Fourth of July? Memorial Day?
And with a little history, a few references, and a lot of intuition,
we'd adjust our weekly bake plan. For example, on Monday of
the previous week we might have sold six hundred cupcakes. If
this upcoming Monday there was a convention in town, we'd
plan to do another six hundred and have an extra fifty just in
case. We worked hard to get the bake plan down to a science.
Nowadays, we probably have no more than eighteen cupcakes
left at the end of an average day.

Perfecting the menu—and determining which flavors were
most popular—was another challenge entirely. We'd started
with twenty-two recipes, and some became instant favorites
while others took a while to catch on. Interestingly, I didn't have
our all-time best seller on the menu when we opened.

One day a guy came in and peered into the case, studying all the various flavors we had for sale that day. I asked

if he needed help, but he just kind of shushed me. Finally he looked up.

"Where's your white on white? Your vanilla-vanilla?"

"Oh, I don't have one of those," I said kind of sheepishly.

He looked offended. "What are you talking about? You gotta make one."

I was a little flustered, but I'm nothing if not resourceful. I decided to show him some real on-the-spot Gigi creativity.

"Okay. Give me a minute."

I went in the back, took a vanilla cupcake, swirled it up with white buttercream, and put white nonpareils on top. I took it out to the guy. He looked stunned that I'd whipped up exactly what he was looking for.

"Here you go, sir," I said, smiling sweetly. "Gigi's Wedding Cake."

He bit into it and flipped. "Now, THAT's what I'm talking about!"

After he left we dove back into the kitchen and made three trays of our newest cupcake—and we sold every single one.

Today, Wedding Cake is our best seller across the entire Gigi's system—17.7 percent of our sales on a daily basis are Wedding Cake. We've sold more than seventeen million of them. Somebody even figured out that if you put every Wedding Cake we've sold since 2009 in a line starting in New York City it would run off the pier in Galveston, Texas. Ironically, it's also our cheapest cupcake to make—originally it cost about seventy-two cents to make. There's no fruit, nuts, or chocolate; it's just vanilla cake and vanilla frosting with some white nonpareils on top.

My mom was very involved at this stage of the company's evolution, and we had a great time trying new things out, experimenting, and adapting old family recipes. It was fun using my customers as guinea pigs, because their taste buds helped determine what we kept and what we discarded.

We felt a little like trendsetters, and I guess in a way we were. I wanted each cupcake to have its own personality, to be its own little work of art. We did a maple-bacon cupcake way before putting bacon in desserts was popular, even candying our own bacon in the back. We did an Oreo cupcake before other people were doing it. We whipped up a chocolate-malt cupcake. I took my great-aunt Ruby's sheet cake recipe, put some chocolate decorations on it, topped it with a yellow fondant star, and dubbed it Texas Milk Chocolate. And one of my all-time triumphs as a baker made its debut around this time: the Kentucky Bourbon cupcake, a luscious bourbon-flavored cake with pecan pie–style filling and chocolate chips with a bourbon cream cheese frosting.

Scarlett's Red Velvet was a classic Southern recipe, much richer and creamier than regular ol' red velvet cake. I loved it but didn't initially see how popular it would become. I got set straight one night when I was working the counter shortly before closing time.

There was a long line of people grabbing some goodies on their way home, and we were working our way through the orders quickly and efficiently. A woman came up to the counter and told me she'd driven an hour from Clarksville to get her Gigi's fix. I thought that was terrific—a super-customer!

She said, "I'd like a half dozen Scarlett's Red Velvet cupcakes."

Oops. "Oh, I'm so sorry. I didn't bake those today."

Her smile vanished. She started yelling at me like I'd just insulted her mama. "Are you kidding me?! *You didn't bake them?!*"

"Ma'am, I'm so sorry."

"How could you not bake them?" she shouted. "You should bake them every day!"

The other customers were watching to see what I was going to do. One said, "Hey, chill out. It's just a cupcake."

The woman was shocked. "It's *not* just a cupcake! *It's Scarlett's Red Velvet!*"

As I was digesting this, I boxed up a half dozen assorted cupcakes and handed them to her.

"Ma'am, I hope this will do for now. I promise next time there'll be red velvet cupcakes here. You have my word."

That seemed to mollify her. "Okay, then. I'll be back on Friday."

I realized I was on to something. Most people would have gone back to the kitchen and cried. But I was considering another angle. This lady was ready to cuss me out because I didn't have her favorite cupcake. I was so excited. Yelling at me over a cupcake! Amazing. *Cha-ching!* I had struck cupcake gold.

I went home that night and made a menu that included rotating flavors. The woman from Clarksville had been right. In her own way, she'd been telling me she'd found something very special that she loved, and she expected consistency. People wanted consistency. Scarlett's Red Velvet went on the menu three days a week, and it became wildly popular, with regular customers planning which days they could come in and get it. I had a printed menu made, and I also put it on our website at GigisCupcakesUSA.com.

Each day we'd have a slightly different menu, but clearly some things should be available every day, like Wedding Cake. I realized that if we didn't have Wedding Cake all the time, we'd lose huge sales and wouldn't have a business for very long. Same for Midnight Magic and White Midnight Magic, our scrumptious gifts to chocolate fiends everywhere. So a menu lineup of staples evolved during the first year, which gave our customers consistency and regularity they could count on.

Determining which flavors and recipes could work on a seasonal basis was an exercise in trial and error. But we could see what other culinary businesses were doing—a lot of market research had already been done in this area. Certain things would sell at certain times of the year—we just had to figure out how to translate that into "cupcakese." I read somewhere that Starbucks learned they had to have pumpkin spice lattes in September or they might as well just shut their doors. So I started adding my own fall variants, like apple pie and pumpkin spice latte cupcakes. I found that people don't want pumpkin after Thanksgiving; as December dawns they're ready for holiday flavors. So we did a holiday menu for a couple months, and then in the spring found we couldn't sell anything wintry. We discovered that as the weather warmed up, people generally liked fruitier flavors— lemon, coconut, lime, etc.

It evolved. And I found the whole thing fascinating. I've

always loved data and statistics—what people are buying or not buying, what flavors and colors are popular or unpopular, what drives somebody to buy something.

Mom became intrigued by the idea of "specialty" cupcakes. Together we did a butter rum cupcake with a little fondant snow angel on a field of powdered sugar snow. Then we did a version with a sugarplum and purple sugar. It was great fun for us as bakers and for our customers, who oohed and aahed when we put the seasonal and specialty cupcakes out.

One day an employee came in to pick up her check. I was fiddling with a new recipe in the kitchen, so I hijacked her to do some taste-testing.

I handed her a bronze-looking cupcake. She bit into it and her face went slack. "Oh my gosh. This is the best thing I've ever put in my mouth. What is it?"

"It's our new peanut butter cupcake: milk chocolate with a little bit of cinnamon and peanut butter cups."

She wolfed it down. "This is mind-blowing."

My mom had an idea for a lemon poppy seed cupcake with a lemon drizzle on top. It was delicious, but I didn't think the drizzle was a worthy substitute for the Gigi swirl. Customers were getting used to my tall frosting—it was my shtick.

"Mom, they don't sell. People want frosting."

"Well, but this is so delicious without all that frosting. It's your dad's favorite."

I said, "I know, but this isn't about what Dad likes. Not many people come in here looking for poppy seeds. And people eat with their eyes. They don't want a flat cake with a drizzle. That's not what our brand is. But your idea about doing something lemony is good. Let's do a tangy lemon cake with a big lemon swirl and see what happens."

So we went in the back, ditched the poppy seeds, and banged out a new recipe—Lemon Dream Supreme, with tall frosting, lemon pie filling, and a candy lemon slice on top. We put it on the floor the same day. Customers were milling around, so I said, "This is new, everyone."

It was a hit.

I still do that occasionally. I'll go in the back and come out with a tray of something new, and customers will get curious.

"What's that?"

"Well, it's the best thing you'll ever put in your mouth, that's what it is," I'll declare. "It's brand-new. I just designed it. Go ahead and try one."

And then they usually order a dozen.

We were starting to catch a wave.

- - - - -

As Gigi's took off and we struggled to keep up with demand, I started working closer with Bryan, my food purveyor.

"I need more butter. And next delivery, I need more powdered sugar."

"Good grief," he'd say. "I thought I'd only sell you ten bags a month, not ten bags a week."

"Bryan, I'm going to need twenty bags this week."

"Twenty bags? What are you doing over there?"

I laughed. "Selling lots of cupcakes. It's just going crazy. And those little vanilla bottles—they're not working for me. It's killing me financially. I need a big jug of vanilla."

"McCormick makes it in a quart."

"Okay. We'll take quarts but that won't last me. I'm going to need a gallon."

"Well, no one sells vanilla by the gallon."

"Somebody does."

"Let me check into it."

About this time my brother Randall came on board, and he overheard this conversation. He went off and did some research and came back with a solution.

"There are several extract companies that sell by the gallon. Lochhead Manufacturing Company is one of the best. Apparently they make the best pure vanilla around."

I was jazzed. "Great, tell them I want my own Gigi's brand vanilla."

"It's going to cost you."

"I know. But I want something special."

For six months we worked with Lochhead to create a custom Gigi's vanilla that would be unique—perfectly sweet and balanced, something that would complement all our ingredients and work in all our recipes. I tasted a zillion variations until I found one that I liked. It was worth the extra effort, because once we'd found it, everything seemed to get a little tastier—a reminder that quality is always worth fighting for.

The day we got our first shipment of extract from Lochhead, I opened up the shipping container, took out the first gallon bottle of vanilla with its customized pink Gigi's label, cradled it in my arms like a newborn baby, and cried. I was so, so happy.

- - - - -

Once things got rolling, we took a deep breath and started fully fleshing out the image of the company. We had a cool logo, I'd picked a vibrant corporate color scheme of pinks and greens, and I'd created a clean, modern look for the store. But we needed marketing materials, brochures, packaging, and images for ads, press use, and catalogs. Our menu was serviceable, but it was kind of cheap and amateurish-looking. I knew we could do better.

I did a couple of photo shoots featuring me with a dazzling spread of cupcakes and photogenic little girls as my kitchen sidekicks. The photographer had me put on an apron and pretend I was eating a cupcake, and that shot became the first big picture that would go up in all our stores. We also shot my first "founder" picture—me holding up a tray of my new margarita cupcakes. We used the pictures for publicity and made them available to newspapers and magazines every time they did an article on me or the shop.

We finally had the financial resources available to get real packaging made—high-quality boxes and bags and napkins and all the other goodies that customers would get with a visit to Gigi's Cupcakes. I was determined to have quality packaging to go with our quality cupcakes.

I also believed we needed to be branded well. My three favorite brands were Victoria's Secret, Martha Stewart, and Tiffany. Each had its own signature elements. For example, anyone who sees the robin's egg blue box knows it's from Tiffany, and any woman in the world is going to want what's in it. Subconsciously she knows it's classy and very special. I wanted people to have that same feeling about Gigi's—and I wanted them to anticipate the joy they'd have opening the box and revealing what was inside. I wanted my packaging to evoke the same effect as a Tiffany's box. I wanted each item that went out my door to be a special gift.

We needed a design company that could mock up what I had in mind. We went to a meeting down on Music Row with a couple of marketing wizards. They showed us some options, and although the designs were nice, none really met the standard I was looking for.

So I drew a box on a legal pad and said, "I want this. Can you do it?"

They were a little taken aback. "Well, that's not a normal 'retail' approach . . ."

I said, "Good. I want it to look like a gift, not a normal retail item. It needs to make you feel like you're getting a present— that it's not just a box of stuff from a bakery."

They finally locked into what I wanted and mocked it up. It was perfect. Now we needed to find somebody to make them. I wanted to make everything in America.

We did some research and eventually found McCowat-Mercer Packaging, a great old manufacturing company in Tennessee that had been around for about 140 years. So Alan and I hit the road to Jackson, where the McCowat-Mercer guys gave us a tour around their factory and showed off a cross section of the products they made. It was all excellent quality, very impressive. Most important, they were comfortable tackling a smaller idiosyncratic project like Gigi's Cupcakes.

Their main sales guy, Tom Brady, ran through some options for us, all of which we liked. But it quickly became clear that we'd have to take a significant risk to get into business with them. McCowat needed a minimum order of $50,000 to set up the machinery and an initial order of fifteen thousand boxes. To be honest, I was scared to death. There was something inside me that feared we'd buy all these boxes and then never sell another cupcake. What would I do with fifteen thousand cupcake boxes?

But Alan and I kicked it around and decided to be optimistic—we told ourselves we'd go through fifteen thousand boxes in no time. So we tentatively made plans to order what we called a "one-box," a "four-box," a "six-box," and a "twelve-box," each referring to the number of cupcakes a box could hold.

The factory guys asked, "Don't you need a two-box?"

I said, "Nope, we don't want a two-box. Let's do four-boxes, it'll be cheaper than paying for ones and twos and fours. If somebody orders more than one cupcake, they might want two or three or four. A four-box can handle any of that, and it's one less SKU to worry about."

Tom and Alan both thought that made sense. But as Alan and I drove home we fretted. How would we come up with $50,000?

At one point we stopped at a Taco Bell.

I said to Alan, "Hey, can we write this off? Can I pay this with our credit card?"

"Sure, this is a business trip."

"Good. Then I'm going to stick it to the man."

Then I realized, "Wait a minute—I *am* the man."

Alan laughed for months about this, and he told the story to anybody who'd listen. I was happy to provide him with such rich comedic material.

Later, Tom told us the owner of McCowat had both liked our

pitch and believed I'd be a good client if I could just get off the launchpad.

Tom told him, "Bless her heart. How is she ever gonna pull this off? If she scrapes together fifty thousand dollars, I guess we can take her money, but fifty thousand dollars to make these high-end boxes? She is crazy."

The owner shook his head. "You think she'll even sell a thousand of them?"

FYI: seventy-five million boxes later, they're really happy with me!

But at the time they didn't yet understand where I was headed. We had a good shtick—the best cupcakes you'll ever taste—and our packaging had to be just as special. Throughout this first growth spurt I was constantly tinkering, developing the colors, design ideas, logos, and emblems—trying to coax forth what everything was going to look and feel like. And once McCowat-Mercer started making the packaging, I stuck to my guns, especially when people close to me would try to steer me to cheaper off-the-rack methods. I wanted to do it all the right way, even if it was a little more expensive. I instinctively understood that for every dollar we spent branding the company properly we'd probably make back two from customers who bought into the image we would create.

God was at work, showing me the way and giving me access to everything I'd need. For instance, I knew it was no coincidence that Alan's wife, Darlene, was a gifted graphic designer. She'd helped design materials for Ruby Tuesday, and she and I hit it off. Once we'd settled on working with McCowat, she jumped in to help design our menus and brochures and posters.

We'd kick ideas around together and got in a pretty good creative groove. Over the years we designed a seasonal Halloween "Boo Box," a "Smooch Box" for Valentine's Day, and special boxes for spring, Easter, and Christmas. The holiday-themed "Jingle Box" that Darlene and I cooked up is still one of Gigi's top sellers every year.

– – – – –

As we began our expansion effort during the summer of 2008, Alan and I worked out the bugs as to how a Gigi's Cupcakes shop should operate—here's how you staff it, here's the equipment you need, here's what it needs to look like, here are the recipes, here's a food purveyor, here's how much butter and powdered sugar you're going to need, and so forth.

I developed a detailed checklist we could hand to each new store manager and say, "Do this and you'll be fine—you'll make a thousand cupcakes a day without making yourself crazy." We'd done the hard part—proved the concept—and now we were ready to share it with the world.

In November and December we opened our second and third stores just outside Nashville, a store I paid for and owned myself in Cool Springs, and our first franchised store that my parents and my brother Steve opened in Spring Hill, respectively. They put their own money up, and though I was happy they could get in on the action as franchise owners, I wasn't sure Spring Hill would be a good location because the town was too small; the area was growing, but I worried it couldn't support a specialty cupcake store. But Mom and Dad were determined, so I did everything I could to help make it a success.

Our first franchise fee was $25,000. All our franchise partners paid the fee and took the risk on their store, including the build-out, buying our specified equipment, and providing proper training. In late 2008 and early 2009 it cost about $175,000 all-in to open a new franchise store. Today, it's more like $275,000.

Another was opened by a guy from Chattanooga who'd just sold his company, had money to play with, and wanted to do something new and fun. He was probably the biggest man I'd ever seen; I'd guess he was six-six and 450 pounds.

He said, "I'm really not the type of guy you want as the face of a cupcake operation."

I shrugged. "Well, just don't stand up front and scare all the customers away."

We had a good laugh, and to tell you the truth, we were both worried about him eating up all his profits. He really loved my cupcakes and could power down three or four in one sitting.

Things got kind of crazy pretty quickly. I was getting calls all the time from people who'd heard we were franchising. I remember negotiating with a franchise candidate while I was cleaning a house for one of my longtime clients. I had to shout over the vacuum cleaner.

Alan was thrilled with the initial response, but he was worried that my attention was divided. I was still trying to juggle the cleaning company while Gigi's Cupcakes took shape, and I guess my seams were starting to show.

"Gina, you need to clear your schedule so you can meet with these people who want to open their own stores. If you want to grow the company, you have to be more available."

I was excited, but a little scared, too. "Things are moving pretty fast. I don't know if I want to grow this much this quickly."

He sighed. "Well, we kind of already are. It might be a little too late to stop the momentum. People are absolutely howling for franchises."

We didn't have the money to proactively market the idea or to do any serious analysis or research about potential markets. There was no master plan. We'd just answer the phone and find out that somebody wanted one. People were interested based upon their own experiences at a Gigi's, or they heard about the franchising opportunity through the grapevine.

The couple from Indianapolis came back in, and this time I was ready for them. They wound up opening three stores in Indiana.

Alan built his own store in Huntsville. We added Athens, Georgia, and Montgomery, Alabama, and suddenly I was spending lots of time in the office meeting people and going on the road to help pick out sites. Our first steps were modest—B and C markets, mostly—because we didn't have enough money or momentum to enter A markets just yet. We knew it would cost a lot more to open a Gigi's in a major city.

It kind of just grew week by week, by word of mouth. More and more franchise candidates appeared. We'd only take about one of every twenty-five seriously; either I wouldn't have a good gut feeling about them, or they lacked money or passion, or both. Eventually I developed a sixth sense about whom we should work with.

I'd say, "Alan, no—these people aren't going to do well."

"Well, they've got the money."

And sometimes I'd give in because my experience in high finance was nonexistent. For example, a millionaire came in one day wanting to buy his twentysomething daughter a shop. She acted entitled, and I could just feel that she wasn't going to work hard or take this seriously.

I told Alan I didn't want to proceed with them.

"Oh, no," he countered. "It'll work. You gotta trust me on this one. This guy's a financial whiz."

I withdrew my objection. I was winging it, operating off my gut and my emerging instincts, but in the end, I was right. The store did gangbuster business right out of the gate like all new Gigi's shops, but then the daughter got bored and let everything slip. Instead of working hard, she'd skip out to get her nails done or go to the movies. Within two years they were almost out of business, so we found another guy to buy them out.

As we hurtled toward the end of our second year in business, we had opened a dozen stores—and the Gigi's empire had taken flight.

- - - - -

Right as we were getting the franchise operation up and running, a young guy named Adam came into the Broadway store. He was kind of nervous, but he looked me right in the eye. He said, "I want to bake. I know you're expanding and I want to be a part of it."

He caught me a little off guard. "Well . . . I'm about ready to open another store. I need some more help around here, that's for sure. Let me train you and we'll see what you can do."

So I started teaching him all my techniques—baking, order-ing, operating the store, you name it. He was a quick learner, and as I watched him, it dawned on me just how important it was going to be to have a bulletproof training function to make sure every Gigi's store had competent employees on staff.

Training was something that I hadn't thought much about, but suddenly it seemed super important. We'd made commit-ments to service all our new franchisees, and within a few months there would be a hundred or more people out there running our businesses. It was an area we needed to take command of.

I put Adam in the manager's chair at the new Cool Springs store. And as we brought other stores online, he began training the employees for the new Gigi's franchises. One after another the teams would come into town, sometimes as many as fifteen at a time, and we'd show them the ropes. Randall was particu-larly good at helping set everything up. He organized training schedules and set up "classes" for trainees. We quickly per-fected a rolling capability to get them ready for battle. As the total number of stores zoomed from three to twelve to thirty-five, we made sure they did everything right.

While Alan and I were off running our stores, expanding the business, and dealing with the everyday needs of our customers, my mom and dad were busy establishing their Spring Hill store. One of their hires, Olga Munera, wanted to become a trainer. I liked Olga and I liked the idea—mostly because I needed help, and because she was terrific.

Mom and Dad balked. "She's our favorite person."

"Let me have her. She doesn't want to be in Spring Hill any-more. She wants to go on the road and grow with the company."

They relented, and soon Olga was out on the road most weeks with either me or Babbs or Randall.

Originally I thought I'd be able to personally attend the grand opening of every new Gigi's Cupcakes. But during the first rush of franchise deals, we were opening two or three stores a week, and I couldn't be in two places at once. As with everything, we scrambled to find a solution.

At that time, we also hired a guy named Mike Huff to help with build-outs, training, and store openings. (He'd later be known as the "Baby Whisperer" after my daughter, Kendel Skye, was born, because he was the only guy who could calm her when she started squawking. He'd curl up with her while he worked on his laptop, and soon she'd be dozing peacefully. He'd put her on his shoulder and bounce her around the office while we worked, which would buy us all a little quiet time. I thought Mike was worth his weight in gold!)

The team took shape and really started clicking. I'd go north with Babbs to open one store. Randall and Olga would head west to open a second, and Mike and Adam would go south to open a third. It was exhilarating.

It seemed like we learned something new every week. In Chattanooga on opening day, in the middle of a downpour, there was a line around the block of eager people waiting under umbrellas to get their first Gigi's cupcakes. At that point in the evolution of our store opening operation, we'd teach new store employees how to create my signature swirl on-site, and that day Adam and I worked with the new Chattanooga staff to madly frost more than a thousand cupcakes each. By the end of the shift, our frosting hands were completely worn out. We both wound up in agony with shooting pains up our arms, and we had to wear braces on our hands for about six months—who knew baking cupcakes could be such a dangerous occupation? My doctor told me the act of creating the swirl actually strained one particular tendon in the thumb, so we developed our own work-around by tucking our thumbs under when we frosted. Another small business hurdle cleared!

Leah had taken over the manager's job at the Broadway store when Babbs started going on the road. I noticed her mind was wandering a bit, and I couldn't quite figure out why—until I realized she was in love! It turned out she'd fallen in love with Adam, who'd originally moved to Nashville from Boston with his fiancée. I could feel a soap opera coming on.

I said to Adam, "You're going to be with Leah. I just know it."

He tried to pretend otherwise, lamely reminding me, "I'm engaged."

"Yeah, well, I hate to tell you, but that's your dream woman right there."

Oh, boy, I thought there was going to be a big drama, but they handled it beautifully. Within a few months the fiancée was out of the picture and Adam and Leah were together. A year after that they were married. I gave serious thought to opening a new division, Gigi's Matchmaking Company, "Baked with Love!"

– – – – –

If you build it, they will come. Or so they said in *Field of Dreams*. Yes, if you make a great product they'll come—but you also have to build a well-rounded business that can survive those slack periods when they don't come. I call it "backdoor business," the weddings and parties and catered events that can often exceed regular walk-in sales. You have to sell cupcakes to people who come to the back door as well as the customers who come in through the front door. The average Gigi's shop can make money on foot traffic, but to reach its fullest financial potential, a store must develop ancillary business.

When a Gigi's first opens, people tend to throng for a few weeks, and everyone is intoxicated by the cupcakes, the variety of flavors, and the sheer joy of indulging the sweet tooth. But after a bit, everyone starts feeling a little guilty for splurging and winds up saying, "Oh, I can't go to Gigi's this week. I'm getting too fat." And that's why you have to have other business models in motion. At my flagship Broadway store, a third of my business is comprised of weddings, corporate clients, medical offices, pharma reps, and other "backdoor" clients like Uber Eats and Grubhub. The other two-thirds of the revenue comes from internet and phone orders and people coming in off the street.

Understanding the rhythms and patterns of your customers' lives and community is important. It took a while to figure out that our slowest months are June and January. June kicks off summer, and summer is all about ice cream and frozen treats. In January people don't want to eat cupcakes because they're "sweeted out" from the holidays, and many are on New Year's resolution diets. I wish I could make them understand that I still have to pay my bills in January—and that we have a low-fat, seventy-two-calorie angel food cupcake that will allow them to splurge a little without busting their diet!

In November we wind up closing for the long Thanksgiving holiday, and even though that covers Black Friday, we found that unless you're in a shopping mall overrun with crazy bargain hunters, it's tough to sell cupcakes that day. We sat through a few Black Fridays and made $200 or $300 before we realized it was much cheaper just to take the day off. Plus, people want pies on Thanksgiving, not cupcakes. We experimented with apple and pumpkin pie–flavored cupcakes—"Not your mama's ordinary pie!"—and did a huge push for a new scrumptious Southern Comfort nine-inch pecan pie. It sold before and after Thanksgiving week, and it did pretty well.

There were so many things to keep track of, so many ideas and concepts that had to be considered and then accepted or rejected. Quality control and consistency emerged as priorities if a Gigi's franchise was going to succeed. I was such a stickler about maintaining the integrity of our menu and our recipes. What we made and served was the basis of our reputation, and it established the terms of our informal contract with our customers. As long as we kept making stellar cupcakes in a clean and welcoming environment, sold them at a fair price, and offered enough variety to keep people interested, Gigi's would remain a special destination where people would come in and treat themselves. Sticking to this formula meant discarding lots of ideas that might have worked somewhere else but were just not a good fit for Gigi's. For instance, you couldn't open a Gigi's franchise and say, "I think I'm going to make a cheeseburger cupcake." It had to meet the Gigi's standard, fit the culinary profile I'd designed, and ultimately be approved by the company.

But as the stores proliferated, some of the owners wanted to monkey around with our mission objectives for one reason or another. One couple wanted to buy the Florence, Alabama, store. The husband spoke eloquently about the restrictions that his faith placed upon his dietary habits, but his inability to sell anything with alcohol was a deal breaker.

I understood but had to hold the line. "A quarter of our cupcakes are made with bourbon or tequila. We can't just change the recipes."

He asked, "Would you be willing to make an exception?"

I said, "No, I can't. I'm sorry. This isn't about you, but about maintaining a certain level of consistency and quality in our products. The ingredients can't be up for debate—our recipes are what made us famous. It would be like asking McDonald's to start baking their french fries."

Another group of investors came in who were Church of Christ members. Now, I grew up in that denomination, so I understood where they were coming from. But they wanted to make nonalcoholic cupcakes, and I had to shut them down, too.

So we lost a few franchisees, but we held on to the purity of our product. When you're building a system you have to stick to your guns—and never lose sight of what's best for that system, no matter how tempting it might be to compromise even just a little.

I had lots of experience praying hard about how to handle people who wanted to deviate from the mission statement and go in directions I thought wouldn't pan out. For instance, from the minute my parents and Steve opened their Spring Hill store, they were constantly pushing, always chafing at the parameters we insisted they respect.

It seemed like I was always saying, "No, Dad. That's not what's best for the system. I'm trying to build a brand here. It has to be about all of us—not just one store, not one person."

All the great culinary companies and restaurant chains operate on this organizing principle. Standardizing operations and steadiness and reliability are critical. And as we grew bigger each year, my devotion to this principle paid off in many ways.

– – – – –

With rapid growth came sizable growing pains. Staff became a priority—as in, how could we find and develop another generation of quality people who could help grow the business?

There was plenty of turnover, so on the advice of counsel I started having people sign a noncompete agreement. Cupcakes were getting hot, and we knew it was only a matter of time before somebody tried to emulate—or outright swipe—our formula.

When we started requiring the noncompete, a couple of the girls who'd been working for just a few weeks didn't want to sign. I suspected they'd just come to work at Gigi's to "see how it was done," and they confirmed my fears when they rather shamelessly gave me a hard time about it. "We can't sign that because we want to do our own cupcake shop someday."

I said, "Well, go find another place to learn the ropes. This isn't a college course, and I'm certainly not going to pay you to learn all my techniques and secrets only to watch you leave and set up shop across the street."

They left and set up their own shop, which crashed after just a few months. So I guess they didn't learn everything they needed to know after all.

As we grew, we always tried to capture the essence of what made eating a Gigi's cupcake such a satisfying and indescribable experience. Lots of superlatives got tossed around in meetings, in the kitchen, behind the counter, and in the car on road trips. But I never could quite wrap my head around any of them. The "essence" of Gigi's was elusive, like trying to hold running water in your hand.

One day the country music singer David Ball walked into the Broadway shop, took a deep breath, and smiled wide. "Oh my gosh. This aroma reminds me of my grandma's house and everything about her that I loved. What a smell."

I thought that was about the best compliment I'd ever gotten.

He continued, "You're takin' people back in time, puttin' them in touch with things they remember best. No one bakes like this anymore. No one has a grandma that does this anymore."

And I thought, "David is right, that's genius." It was exactly what I'd been looking for.

Smell is the most powerful sense, and there are very few aromas more evocative than the smell of baked goods in a warm kitchen. And if I really were transporting people back into their memories for just a moment or two, then my cupcakes were more than just cupcakes—they were a little piece of what they missed, something that had been lost in the busy back-and-forth of modern life.

In 2008 cooking wasn't yet the widespread and fashionable avocation it was about to become. Not many people made fresh, homemade desserts. The foodie revolution had gotten started, but baking wasn't quite cool then.

But I wondered: What if the lasting impressions of grandmothers working in their kitchens could be revived and made popular again? What if I could make Gigi's Cupcakes the old/new, classic/sexy thing? Could my offerings become retro cool tools for the modern woman?

Not everybody understood where I was coming from. I was already selling women something that wasn't, strictly speaking, good for them—if they ate too many cupcakes they'd get fat. But they kept buying them. Why? The answer was that, along with the strong pull of memory that David Ball alluded to, a beautiful, delicious cupcake—not too sweet, not too obnoxious—was a treat a woman could buy for herself. Sure, she'd buy 'em for her kids and coworkers and clients, but sometimes she'd buy it just for herself—a guilty pleasure, or a reward for getting through another day or week, or maybe just a quick getaway from all the mundane things people usually consume. Sometimes a cupcake was more than a cupcake. Wedding Cake was more than a snack—its name and appearance evoked images of bliss and harmony and romance. It was like a whole fairy tale you could hold in your hand.

I was making cupcakes a kind of accessory, a lifestyle thing. Two a week—it's a balance. A guilty pleasure? Certainly. But a modest one—it's not a whole cake, after all, just a taste. Do your walks, go to yoga class, drink water. Then have a treat. Have a Gigi's cupcake. Because guess what? It's so good, it's worth the calories. You deserve it.

Deep inside I knew people craved them. We just needed to

create a mini-movement so women would feel like experiencing one every week or so. Eighty-six percent of our customers are women between the ages of twenty-five and forty-five. Ninety-six percent love lots of frosting—these are the people who want to eat the corner piece of the wedding cake that has the big frosted rose. And they want to be supermoms who know where to get supertreats. Which is why we started focusing on specialty items to keep giving them new things to try: mini-cupcakes, Easter boxes, lush oatmeal cookies, our Christmas Jingle Box.

"Look at these special gifts, everyone. I didn't do them. Gigi's did. And they're just down the street and they're our special treat. Gigi's is our destination. We don't do Kroger. We don't do Publix. We do Gigi's." A woman may not bake cupcakes herself, but she trusts Gigi's to deliver the goods. In other words, she cares enough to get the very best.

Eventually this idea would emerge in 2013 as a major marketing and imaging push, and it became the centerpiece of our biggest expansion to date—a period that saw the company grow from 55 stores to more than 120. We firmly established that Gigi's cupcakes were part of a desirable lifestyle, a quality item that reflected and conferred status and taste. The idea caught on, and I loved that everyone began to agree that my cupcakes were special!

It wasn't just affluent people who bought into this idea. There was a homeless lady who became a regular. One day she came in and fished out four dollars from a threadbare linen bag.

She said, "I don't have a job right now and I'm living in a halfway house, but I do work part-time. I save up once a week so I can come get a cupcake because I know it'll make me feel better."

And I said, "Thank you. You really mean that?"

She nodded. "It makes me feel like everything's going to be okay."

I thought I was going to cry.

There is definitely something unusual about the cupcakes. They don't taste like they were made by a company. Everything about them tastes fresh. They're not too sweet, and the flavors are bold and intoxicating. Someone once told me it must be like what cats feel when they get ahold of some catnip. And each cupcake is a completely different experience, which is exactly what we wanted to achieve. My goal was to create a party in your mouth. You can only get there by completely going for it and by holding nothing back. If you're going to bake an orange cupcake, you've got to have cream and essence of orange in there so it tastes like the orange dreamsicle you ate as a kid. Like David said, it takes you back!

– – – – –

When people came in I'd ask, "Where y'all from? Have you ever had a Gigi's cupcake?"

Newbies tended to look around curiously and politely shake their heads no.

"Your life is about to begin. You're about to have a Gigi's cupcake."

Now, most people were usually not immediately impressed. I mean, everybody's had a cupcake before, right? How good could it be?

So I'd just put a cupcake on the counter in front of them and watch as they'd lift a Wedding Cake or a Red Velvet or a Midnight Magic to their lips, knowing that they still didn't quite get it. They'd take a bite, letting the flavors unfold as they chewed. Then their eyes would usually widen, and the beginnings of a smile would appear. Sometimes there would even be a little moan.

Finally, the punch line would come, almost always delivered in a low, incredulous, almost conspiratorial tone: "Oh my gosh. This is incredible (or amazing, or unbelievable). This is the best cupcake I've ever tasted in my life!"

And that's when I'd know for sure that I'd done my job.

Without getting too mushy about it, I really do think that there's something divine in all this. I believe that when God favors someone, He changes their mind, He opens their eyes, and He touches their heart so they'll be receptive to a wider truth—and then they'll share that truth. I certainly feel like I found His favor. People have welcomed and embraced my vision, and I believe it's because God has blessed me in a thousand ways for many, many years. I think He put the tools in my hands and gave me the chance to move my life and my work in the right direction. And sometimes I wonder if He thinks I've made the world a sweeter place by selling what I feel in my heart—*love*—one cupcake at a time.

I can only hope.

- - - - -

I developed an approach to order and precision and cleanliness that I know has its roots in my previous career as a professional cleaner.

When I go into a bakery or a deli and the case is empty or otherwise forlorn-looking, I always wonder, "Are they too lazy or cheap to keep the case full?" It's a bit of a negative feeling, an uneasiness—"Why are they out of shrimp? Don't they have any more? Are they disorganized? Did they not order enough? Is it old? Has it been sitting there a long time?"

People react the exact same way with cupcakes. If the trays in the case are full, it's satisfying for a customer to go window-shopping and pick out which cupcake she wants. So we always have full trays, and the cases are always clean. My biggest pet peeve is chocolate chips or sprinkles all over the trays. I can't stand the sloppiness.

I'll say to the staff, "What's my biggest pet peeve?"

"You don't like crumbs and sprinkles everywhere?"

"Exactly. And you know what to do, right?"

"Yes, ma'am."

My other pet peeve is just basic cleanliness. Some restaurant chains care a lot about that. Whenever I go into a McDonald's or a Chick-fil-A, they're always clean as a whistle. Cleanliness is important.

About the time I had twenty-two stores, I was out on the road with Babbs and was giving my cleanliness lecture to one of our new store teams. I pulled on my pink rubber gloves and pointed to the back.

"Okay, everyone. We're going to the bathroom. I'm going to show you how to clean. Because whether you're aware of it or not, when you go into someone's bathroom, you'll learn a lot about who they are and what they care about. And if you go into a restaurant bathroom and it's filthy, I can guarantee that the kitchen's probably not that clean, either. Messiness equals carelessness. Remember that. Now follow me."

As we trooped into the semi-dirty bathroom, I clucked a little and pointed out areas that needed improvement.

One of the teenagers whined, "This is beneath me."

I laughed. "Beneath you? Honey, I'm the founder of this company. My name's on the building. And I'm cleaning this toilet. Nothing is beneath you. If you want to succeed in life, roll up your sleeves and do the job in front of you, because somebody is probably watching. And if that means cleaning this toilet until it's spick-and-span, then that's what you've got to do. I have twenty-two stores and I'm perfectly happy to clean this bathroom right now."

She blinked. "You want me to clean the toilet?"

"Bingo." I tossed her a sponge and reminded her, "One day you might own a business yourself, and trust me when I say you'll remember this lesson."

She nodded. "Yes, ma'am."

– – – – –

As we reached the end of our second year, everything had ramped up exponentially. We were opening new stores, developing new recipes, launching marketing and sales campaigns, hiring and firing and training people at a brisk clip . . . it was 100 miles an hour every day. I always felt every morning that there was more to be done that day than I could ever possibly do—I never seemed to get all the way through my daily list of tasks.

I was stretched thin, and everyone in my life noticed. Gigi's

Cupcakes had entered a critical period of growth, but I was still devoting a significant percentage of each day to Gigi's Cleaning Company, which I'd held on to for dear life as an additional cash machine.

Alan took me aside and said, "Gina, it's time for you to stop cleaning houses. We need you here to do far more important things now."

He was right, of course. I knew I had to let go.

I had four girls working for me at the time, we were cleaning about eighty-five houses a week, and there was a local guy who was interested in buying the company from me. But he wanted a detailed business plan, financials, and a formal deal offer, and he wanted me to commit to training staff. I realized I had no time for any of that, so I passed.

I prayed about it one night, and then decided to disperse the cleaning company among my girls. I couldn't think of a better way to hand an opportunity to these women, some of whom had battled poverty, drugs, jail, and abusive spouses.

I sat them all down one morning. "I can't clean anymore. I've got to focus on cupcakes now. But I'm going to give each of you a part of the company so you can all be owners."

They said, "No, no, don't leave . . . we love you."

I said, "You guys are doing a great job and you each have about twenty customers. I want to empower you. I want you to take your clients and make your own business now."

They were scared. None of them had ever done anything even remotely like this.

I said, "I'll help you set it up, but I have to stop pretty soon."

So I put together a plan for them, writing everything down

so they'd know how to do it. I personally wrote letters and called every customer. Some were grateful. Some were mad. But most understood.

One of my longtime cleaning clients was a really cool dermatologist who had two equally cool sisters. When I dropped by to explain what was happening, they were excited for me. So much so that the sisters bought a franchise and opened a Gigi's in Murfreesboro. Then their brother built the two Gigi's stores in Raleigh. I went from cleaning their floors to selling them franchises—a perfect segue!

It was time to move on.

- - - - - - - - - -

Lessons for Life and Business

Don't be afraid to follow your gut instincts. When you listen to your heart, it often leads you back to something precious that you already know but may have forgotten.

TOMATO SPINACH FRITTATA

*T*his is such a healthy and beautiful dish. I'm not much of a breakfast person, but since brunch is such a hip and fashionable thing these days, this recipe will be a hit. It is perfect for when you have guests over for a special occasion or a weekend brunch.

INGREDIENTS

2 tablespoons olive oil

1 garlic clove, minced

One (6-ounce) package fresh baby spinach

One (10-ounce) can Ro*Tel tomatoes, drained

$1/4$ teaspoon salt

$1/4$ teaspoon black pepper

One (4.5-ounce) can sliced mushrooms

12 large eggs, beaten

$1/2$ cup crumbled feta cheese

$1/2$ cup shredded mozzarella cheese

- Preheat the oven to 350°F.

- Heat the oil in a 10-inch (2 inches deep) ovenproof, nonstick skillet over medium heat.

- Add the garlic and sauté for 1 minute, or until fragrant.

- Stir in the spinach and cook for 1 minute, or until the spinach begins to wilt.

- Add the tomatoes, salt, and pepper, stirring frequently for 2 to 3 minutes.

- Add the mushrooms.

- Add the eggs and sprinkle with the cheeses and stir.

- Cook for 3 to 5 minutes, gently lifting the edges of the frittata with a spatula and tilting the skillet so the uncooked portion flows underneath.

- Place the skillet in the oven and bake for 12 to 15 minutes, or until golden brown.

- Remove from the oven and let stand for 5 minutes.

- Slide the frittata onto a large platter and cut into 8 wedges.

FINDING TRUE LOVE

- - - - - - - - - - - - - - -

The Secret Ingredient of Real Happiness

As Gigi's Cupcakes took off, I crossed a personal threshold. Although I certainly was proud of my professional accomplishments and was ready and willing to do whatever I could to grow my company, I kind of went into my shell after the first burst of publicity and celebrity. I discovered that, despite my past willingness to take the stage as a singer or walk into an office to fight for my ideas, deep down I was actually fairly shy. Suddenly there I was on TV and in newspapers and magazines, being held up as some sort of inspirational rags-to-riches character. Everywhere I went, people wanted to hear my story, and every day I found myself interacting with strangers who walked into my store or stopped me on the street.

It was gratifying on one level, but unnerving on another. I don't mean to say I had stage fright or an aversion to doing my thing in public. It was just dawning on me that my Gigi's persona was strong, confident, and successful, which was the opposite of how I felt in my real world. I still hadn't overcome some basic hurdles in my private life, and I knew there was work to be done.

For years, whenever I'd go into a bar or a restaurant, the first thing I'd think would be, "Oh, I'm fat and ugly, no one will like me, no one will want to be my friend," or, "There are so many nice-looking guys in here, but none of them will be interested in somebody like me." I suppose it was my way of insulating myself against the pain of rejection, and I tried to convince myself that I didn't care. But of course I did care.

Now, even as I was becoming a public figure of sorts, that virus was still in me—I could still occasionally find myself paralyzed by an almost juvenile fear of not being accepted. No matter how I tried to rationalize it away, I knew deep down inside it had something to do with my humble origins, and the very real class divide I could feel in the world around me. I was a blue-collar character who'd moved into a white-collar world.

And though I perhaps placed too much emphasis on this gap between "them" and "me" and let it cloud my outlook, as soon as I stopped cleaning houses and founded a burgeoning new corporation, I discovered that it wasn't all in my head. My first exposure to it came when one of my wealthy former cleaning customers called me up out of the blue.

"We're having a party, Gigi," she began. "I've been reading about your new business and I was hoping maybe you could cater desserts for us."

Ever eager to develop my "backdoor business," I dove right in. I even felt a little twinge of nostalgia—for old times' sake it might be fun to see some of my old clients again.

Obviously, the rules of the game had changed a little. I was no longer a house cleaner; I was an entrepreneur whose expertise had been sought. But where I expected some basic respect and courtesy, I found only weirdness. When I arrived to set up for the party, right away I felt a certain tension, as if I were still the lowly chambermaid. And it was odd to find myself working again with people whose toilets and dirty laundry I'd once cleaned. I think it was a little awkward for them, too, because while I busily served cupcakes to a party full of people, I overheard plenty of gossip.

"That's the girl who started the cupcake business, right?"

"She used to be the maid, you know."

"The maid?!?"

"She used to mop floors! Now she owns that cupcake place down on Broadway."

"I wonder how she managed to afford that."

"Well, I've heard she has quite an active romantic life, if you know what I mean."

I tried not to let it bother me, but this kind of thing tended to reinforce my insecurities. Intellectually, I knew I wasn't twelve years old anymore and shouldn't let it get to me. So I'd tell myself, "Stop thinking like this—take a deep breath, go live your life, and tune out all this static."

As the pressure at work built up and my workdays grew longer and longer, I was surprised to find that despite having lots of good friends, eager employees, and terrific business associates, I was lonely. I wanted to be in love again. And I knew in my gut that all the success in the world wouldn't mean much if I didn't have someone special to share it with.

All this time I had been seeing Trevor, but it was definitely on-again, off-again. And I realized my relationship with him was at the center of my loneliness. Despite the physical distance between us, we'd managed to carve out a little time together, but the relationship remained superficial and directionless—I couldn't call it healthy or satisfying by any means.

Trevor would come into town regularly, and he'd usually spend most of his time visiting his friends and family. Even though I felt as if I were number two or three on his list, I'd corral him to help me at the shop, go out to dinner, and hang out. We always had fun together—I was still enthralled by him, hanging on his every word, relishing every joke, melting with every touch. But it felt like I was always doing the pursuing, which isn't something any woman wants to do. He always held back, physically and emotionally, so things remained casual, with no strings attached, and we sort of drifted from month to month with no certainty. Were we really in love? Would we stay together? Would he move to Nashville? Would I move to Virginia? I hated myself for going along with it, and I knew I'd have to force the issue eventually.

I was starting to look down the road a bit, thinking about some other goals. And time and again, one particular ambition rose up to fill my field of view. I began to wonder if there just might be enough room in my life to work toward the biggest goal of all.

I wanted to be a mother.

- - - -

During my divorce, I'd suffered various physical ailments, many of which were brought on by the stress and torment of that awful situation. I sought medical care on several fronts and learned that my ability to conceive and bear children was in serious doubt. But I wasn't ready to make peace with the idea of not having children. If in fact I couldn't conceive naturally, what other options did I have?

I did what I usually do: I got out a legal pad and started taking notes, researching, making phone calls, and picking all the brains I could. And this little project led me to determine once and for all whether or not Trevor was going to remain in my life. If I was going to have a child, it would either be with him (my first choice), or through some other means (my second choice, but still a good option).

Despite my ups and downs with Trevor, I believed the chemistry between a man and a woman often cannot be denied. But I still needed to know if I could "fix" him, as silly as that sounds. I loved him and wanted to be with him, even though there had been plenty of warning signs that might have driven another woman away. As it turned out, several opportunities popped up that would help clarify our situation.

In the spring of 2008 I made plans to attend my high school reunion in Quartz Hill. Trevor agreed to go with me, and we mapped out a little romantic getaway in Los Angeles after the reunion. I was looking forward to showing him off to all my old friends and neighbors and telling everyone the exciting story about my new business. But two days before we were scheduled to leave, he told me he couldn't go. He didn't give me a reason, so I sort of snapped and told him if he couldn't go, we were breaking up. I went to California by myself, and the whole trip was very sad.

All I could think of was what might have been, because despite his brutish behavior, it felt as if he still had my heart locked up. I was utterly helpless to stop the feeling. I prayed to God every night to release me from this man—or to change his heart so we could be together. It was all so crazy. I felt like I was losing my mind.

A few weeks after the reunion, the swirl of running the store had lifted my spirits and lightened my mood. And then, out of the blue, Trevor texted me: "Hey, I'm thinking about you. Missing you. I'm in town."

It was obvious what I should have done: not responded. But I let him back in, and of course without even discussing how he had hurt me, I followed his lead and we spent a wonderful few days together. But he still wouldn't talk about the future.

God help me, I was blind. After this visit, I remember breaking down and crying in the bathroom at the shop. I was exhausted, working all the time, and obsessed with this man who clearly knew how I felt yet wouldn't lift a finger to make me feel better.

My friends and family were worried. I was losing sleep, not eating regularly. I was miserable. I tried to explain that when Trevor turned his attention to me, it was like the sun was shining on me. I insisted that he was a better man than he seemed. And I was certain that despite my doubts, Trevor was meant to be part of my destiny. I believed I was supposed to have a child with him.

I'd brought my brother Randall in as COO to work closely with me in launching new properties and training new employees. He was great with people and always perked everybody up when he got going. He and I went to Midland, Texas, to open up a store in October 2009, and I invited Trevor along.

When we got to Midland we were all pretty tired. We checked into the hotel and Trevor fell asleep right away. I sat up reading for a while. Trevor's phone, which was plugged into a charger on my side of the bed, kept buzzing as a string of text messages came in. On the screen I saw "Linda."

A month or so before, Trevor had taken me to Virginia Beach to see his "other" life and get a sense of where he lived. Linda had shown up at his house one night, and he told me she was an ex who was having a difficult time letting go.

So lying there in the hotel room in Midland, I texted her back. "Hey, Linda. Trevor's not your boyfriend anymore. Leave him alone."

But the next morning, while he was in the shower, she started texting him again with a vengeance. She sent pictures of herself posing and smiling, telling him she couldn't wait to see him.

When he came out of the bathroom, I confronted him.

"You're cheating on me, aren't you?"

"No, I'm not cheating."

But I knew what was going on. We got into a huge fight, and he got so mad that he left and flew home. This time I was determined to not worry about Trevor anymore.

But a month later he started texting me again.

I texted back. "Leave me alone."

I tried to ignore him, but a few days later he pushed all my buttons with another text. "I'll be in town after Christmas. How about a romantic New Year's Eve, just you and me?"

And thus began another bumpy chapter. I agreed to see him, and we started texting back and forth. Soon we were back together again, whatever that meant.

Trevor finally moved to Nashville, which I initially took as a sign that he was starting to think long-term about our relationship. He got a job at a jewelry store that a friend of his owned in downtown Franklin and started to make a living buying and selling gold and silver. He lived with his brother but spent a lot of time at my place. We started to feel like a couple, and things went very smoothly for a month or so.

One night I decided to tell Trevor what I really wanted.

"I want to get married. And I want to have a child."

He didn't bat an eyelash. "Well, I don't want to get married. And I definitely don't want another child."

So—incredibly, amazingly—we broke up again.

- - - - -

At this point in my life, I had never owned very many nice things. I'd spent a lot of time working hard to get ahead, but I hadn't taken much time to enjoy the fruits of my labor. Now, with Gigi's Cupcakes up and running, I was starting to make some decent money, and I decided to find a nice place to live. I'd outgrown my little house on Edmondson Pike, and the neighborhood had changed so much so that I put it on the market.

It sold quickly, and I had to move out sooner than I'd planned, so I rented a rambling house on thirteen picturesque acres along Goose Creek. I loved being right on the water, and the property had tons of privacy and was quiet—exactly the kind of refuge I'd always dreamed of.

When I called my parents to tell them about it, my dad was concerned about my ability to keep up such a large place.

"It's just temporary, Dad. And just so you know, I'm going to start enjoying my life a little more. Don't worry, I've got everything under control."

I had noticed a subtle shift in my dealings with my folks. I loved them and valued their opinions, but I was more than ready for them to take a step back and give me a few props for everything I'd accomplished. I thought maybe a little respect was due.

My folks had been generous at several critical junctures— with recipes, interim financing, construction, manpower— you name it; they'd always been ready and willing to help. And though I didn't want to hurt either of them, I also didn't want them telling me how to run my personal life or the business I'd created. I had to gently make sure my veto power was absolute.

— — — — —

A few months later, on May 1, 2010, a massive rainstorm hit Nashville and flooded the city. It made the national news—the Cumberland River overflowed, the Grand Ole Opry wound up half underwater, and waves rolled down the boulevards in downtown Nashville. It was a major disaster, and it caused billions of dollars of damage.

I was working at the cupcake shop when the worst of it hit. After listening to the weather warnings, I decided to close up and send everyone home early—there was no telling what kind of destruction might be headed our way.

I had Prancer with me, and we drove home through the downpour. We turned off the road onto my half-mile-long driveway and plunged right into a swiftly moving stream that hadn't been there when I had left for work that morning. I heard a terrible crunch. The car groaned and died, and I found out later I'd bottomed out the transmission.

As we sat there it started raining harder. The broad, grassy ten-acre front yard disappeared under a thin layer of river water. Then the volume and speed of the flooding suddenly seemed to double.

I tried not to panic. My brother had parked his truck and Jet Ski trailer in my yard, and I knew he had some life jackets stowed in the truck bed. I tucked Prancer under my arm like a football and plunged into the water, which rapidly rose from waist to shoulder level as I waded the hundred yards to the truck. As I fished out a couple of life jackets, the water level reached the Jet Ski, which lifted off the trailer and started bobbing around like a cork.

There was no way to get to my neighbors, who were a half mile away, so I stuck one life jacket on Prancer, then wriggled into the second one. We waded to the house, which was up on a low rise. For the moment, it mercifully sat dry above the flood line.

I looked out to Goose Creek and watched the floodwaters rise. Chairs and bushes and a telephone pole drifted by, along with a bunch of thrashing little moles who'd apparently been flushed out of their holes in the yard. Then, incongruously, a goat floated by.

Within an hour a couple of safety officers in a boat tried to approach but there were still ten acres of rushing river between us. Having gotten my number from the neighbors, they called my phone. They told me to get a couple of days' worth of basics to bring with me. Prancer and I were more than ready to be rescued.

I ducked back into the house to gather some things, but within a minute or two one of the officers talking on his radio started waving through the window at me. "Ma'am, we've got to go. There's an eighty-year-old man stranded up a tree and the water's rising. We got to go get him right now. We'll be back."

As they zoomed away, the water continued to rise all around me. It wouldn't be long before it started flowing right into the house. It was looking as if I was going to have to swim for it.

My cell phone rang. It was Trevor. We hadn't spoken in weeks. I automatically felt a flash of anger as I saw his number come up, but I answered anyway.

He said, "I saw on the news your neighborhood was getting hit pretty hard. How are you doing?"

"Well, I've had better days." Trying hard not to sound freaked, I explained my predicament.

"I'll be right over," he said, sounding very much in command.

A half hour or so later he arrived, along with another vehicle towing a canoe on a trailer. He'd roped one of my neighbors, a retired army guy, into helping him out. It took them nearly two hours to paddle in the canoe against the tide, but they finally reached me, just as the waterline breached my doorjamb and started flooding the house. Prancer and I were saved, and we were rowed to safety. Hallelujah!

Trevor took me to the Residence Inn and got me a room for the night. I realized we had stumbled into a real "My hero!"

moment. Trevor had literally just saved my life. He was very affectionate and attentive. We got some food, had a glass of wine, and one thing led to another. The next morning I woke up in his arms, wondering what I might have just gotten myself into.

We headed back to Goose Creek to get some clothes and other odds and ends. The water was still high. The owner had shown up and was surveying the destruction. There was lots of water damage, but it was repairable. Compared to some people in town who'd been devastated by the flood, I'd gotten off easy. I'd be able to move back in within a week or so.

Finally able to take a deep breath, I looked at Trevor and he looked at me. We both knew it was time to sort things out once and for all. For the next few days we saw each other, and it felt good to me. He seemed a little more flexible, and a little more caring and sensitive, than he had during our last go-round. So eventually we worked our way up to sitting down with a cup of coffee to have "the talk."

"Look, Gina," he said, "I know you want a family, but I just don't want any more kids. That's not where I am in my life."

"I want a family. And I want to be with you. I want to marry you. Don't you want to marry me?"

He sat there for a long moment, considering the question.

"No," he said quietly. "I don't want to marry you. I'm not in love with you."

I swear my heart stopped. "Were you ever in love with me?"

"I love you—but I'm not *in love* with you."

I was crushed. "What about when you said you were going to honor me? What was that all about?"

He shrugged and sipped his coffee. "Look, I just don't want to be with you anymore."

I was stunned, unable to believe that after everything that had gone down between us he could be so callous.

- - - - -

Trevor or no Trevor, I wanted a child. With great difficulty, I closed the door on him, even though I still had strong feelings. I'd gotten into my mid-thirties without finding the kind of stable relationship that I could build a family upon, but I wasn't about to let that stop me.

I saw a fertility doctor and took a bunch of tests. The results were not encouraging, but through meds and a regimen of Clomid injections, it was possible I might conceive.

I prayed about it with my best friend, Susan. The prospect of raising a child as a single mother didn't scare me logistically or financially, but I was concerned about a child not having a father figure in his or her life. It was possible, of course, that I would eventually meet someone and build a family, but I didn't want to wait around for that to happen. Plus, almost no aspect of my life had unfolded traditionally, so I decided to press on and leave the outcome in God's hands. He knew what I needed, what I was capable of, and what was in my heart. I would trust in Him.

I signed up with the Cryobanks sperm bank and bought three samples. I liked the man's genetic profile—smart, athletic, strong. The first effort didn't take. I did a second procedure— and then kept my fingers crossed.

During this period, even though we were broken up, I would talk to Trevor from time to time. I don't know why I couldn't just cut him out of my life, but I couldn't. He told me that he'd been despondent since we'd broken up, and that he'd had second thoughts about how it had ended. I decided not to tell him about my efforts to get pregnant. I really didn't need to hear again that he didn't want to have a child with me.

Then the second insemination effort failed, and I thought, "Well, if I can't have kids, I might as well be with someone that I love." And even though he'd hurt me over and over again, I decided to get back together with Trevor. I still didn't tell him about the fertility efforts; if I couldn't have kids anyway, why did it matter?

Of course, in time I would discover that even after we got back together, he was still running around with Linda behind my back. And when I confronted him, he yet again assured me it was over. I knew I couldn't trust him. But I looked past it all because I still loved him. That was the state of my self-esteem at that point. The Gigi of today wouldn't do that—she'd rather just be by herself.

In August I didn't have a period. I waited a couple weeks and then went to the doctor. And wouldn't you know it? Against all odds, after failing at artificial insemination and battling back from all my previous complications, I was finally, gloriously, happily pregnant—I was going to have a child!

When I finally worked up my nerve to tell Trevor, he was aghast. He couldn't summon even a token bit of happiness or joy or congratulations for me.

"No, that's impossible. I can't have any more kids."

I grinned. "Well, the doctor says I'm pregnant."

I was so happy. But he was determined to ruin the moment.

"It's not mine. Whose is it?"

I finally told him the whole story about my treatments, and how he had unwittingly supplied me with the missing element after all else had failed. This pregnancy was not artificial . . . it was one hundred percent natural. But he couldn't see the upside of any of it.

As my pregnancy progressed, I stayed busy at work, running the company, touring all over the country picking out locations, training employees, opening new stores, and expanding my cupcake empire. Some days I didn't feel great, but I didn't want to show anyone that I couldn't do it all, have it all, and make it all work.

Frankly, I'd thought I'd get some help from Trevor, but those nine months turned out to be very difficult between us. It was an exquisite kind of torture, knowing I was going to have a child soon, but feeling like I had the world on my shoulders with no one to support me. Right or wrong, I'd decided to give Trevor the time and space to come around in his own way to the fact that we were going to have a baby together. I prayed every night that God would give him the strength to recognize this development as a blessing and not a curse, and I held out hope that he'd wind up being the man I believed he could be. But what I saw wasn't very encouraging.

He'd say, "You're gaining lots of weight; you're not going to be attractive to anyone after you give birth. You need to exercise more."

I wanted to hear that I was more beautiful than ever, that there was a special glow around me, that I was Mother Earth herself! I mean, could a guy be more clueless and insensitive?

When I was alone, I let my fears about Trevor and my raging body chemistry overwhelm me. I spent a lot of time crying and wondering if he'd ever start acting like a man and a father.

A few months later we were driving home from a movie and he started in again, accusing me of cheating on him and getting pregnant by another man, of entrapping him.

"This child is a blessing, Trevor. A blessing from God."

"You leave God out of this," he said. "God has nothing to do with this."

We pulled up to a stoplight and he continued berating me.

But I wasn't listening anymore. For the first time since I'd met him I looked at him with completely clear eyes. I saw a petty, mean-spirited, duplicitous creep who only cared about himself, who couldn't muster a modicum of human decency or courtesy for a woman who'd loved him through thick and thin. I was almost eight months pregnant by then, and I thought, "That's it. I'm done."

I got out of the car and started walking home.

– – – – –

During this time I found myself wishing I could find a truly dependable right-hand man, somebody I enjoyed being with who understood who I was and what I needed. Somebody who could be as passionate about Gigi's Cupcakes as I was. And I realized I already had the answer.

You'll recall Brad Harlan. We'd met several years before when he hired me to clean a Grammy winner's house. We'd clicked instantly, and Brad and I promised each other we'd find something else to do together someday.

Brad had gone home to live in Corpus Christi, Texas, but would come into town occasionally. I'd always drag him down to the Broadway store with me, where he'd wind up pitching in. He fit in perfectly, helping customers, cleaning, making cupcakes, organizing this and that. I was so impressed. He was a natural and such a quality guy in so many, many ways.

In 2010 Brad saw on Facebook that I was pregnant. He sent me a sweet message of congratulations. I called him and invited him to a store opening in San Antonio I'd be attending in a few weeks.

So we met for the opening, which turned out to be a hot mess. The franchisees were disorganized, and nothing was together as the grand opening approached. Brad took a look around and dove right in. And he just nailed it. Here I was, four months pregnant, trying to stay on my feet, and more than a little out of my mind. But he sort of took over and executed all my orders, smoothly and professionally, with a smile and cheery attitude—as if we'd been doing this together for years. Somehow the opening wound up being a hit.

Afterward, I told him if he ever moved back to Nashville I'd give him a job at the Broadway store, and that I'd refer him to cleaning customers I used to have until he got his feet on the ground. The next week he packed and moved back.

He went right to work with Leah at the store, and within just a few months his leadership skills and raw creativity had dazzled everyone. Leah was managing the Broadway store at the time, but she and Adam were planning to marry, and she was ready to try something else.

Six months after Brad arrived, Leah and Adam asked to meet me. Leah wanted to move to Cool Springs to help Adam with the training program, and she thought I should give the Broadway store to Brad to manage.

And just like that, I had the right-hand man I'd been wishing for.

– – – – –

On May 29, 2011, everything in my life changed. I was lying in the delivery room at the Vanderbilt University Hospital with tears rolling down my cheeks, and my obstetrician handed me my beautiful, brand-spanking-new baby girl, all wrapped up in a little blanket and looking every inch like the miracle she truly was. And in that instant, I stopped worrying and fretting about so many of the small things that had long bedeviled me.

I let a profound and permanent joy take hold of me. I could feel God in my daughter's warmth and in her breath, and I could see Him in her eyes and her little hands. The enormity of the gift He'd given me was almost too much to bear. I held her tight and prayed in gratitude and humility—and I vowed to protect her and nurture her and help her find her way in a world I would never stop trying to make gentle and kind and welcoming. I whispered a promise that I would do my best to keep her from falling victim to the cruelties and stupidity I'd suffered, and I made a pact to love her and laugh with her and enjoy every moment we would share together. It was the single greatest moment of my life.

It had been a rough night. Even though we were pretty much on the outs, Trevor had stepped up and deigned to accompany me to the hospital. My water broke naturally, but unfortunately I became one of the rare women who falls deathly ill with stomach flu–like symptoms. I couldn't lift my head off the pillow. I went into labor for twelve hours and was in agony, so they decided to give me an epidural. After a while, the delivery staff saw the baby was in distress—the cord was wrapped around her neck—so they quickly performed an emergency C-section. I was scared, so Trevor stayed with me. He was there for me that day.

The next morning I woke up with little Kendel Skye in my arms and realized my biggest dream had come true. But it hit home: I'd just had a child with a man who didn't want a child. As we sat in the room with our new daughter, a young woman in casual clothes came in to deliver the results of a DNA test I'd ordered—so that once and for all we could answer the question of whether or not Trevor was Kendel Skye's father. Personally, I didn't think the test was necessary, because Kendel Skye arrived looking exactly like Trevor—even his own brother remarked on the amazing likeness.

Of course, the DNA test proved that Trevor was Kendel Skye's father. But he still didn't believe it or accept it. Even though we'd broken up, I'd been hoping he'd come around and at least be a good father to his daughter, but it didn't look like it was in the cards.

So I went home alone to my new house with my new baby and started a new life. I was going to raise my daughter and be a happy and fulfilled person. I'd found true love not once, but twice. One had ended in heartbreak. The other had refilled and overflowed that same wounded heart with a kind of devotion I'd never known before but had always longed for.

I knew that, come what may, Kendel Skye would always be mine, and I would always be hers. In the years to come we would celebrate many highs and lows together. And because we were a team, our triumphs and victories would be sweeter, and our defeats would be less painful because we would have each other.

True love at last.

– – – – – – – – – – –

Lessons for Life and Business

I believe we can all find it in ourselves to be genuinely grateful for what we have, for what we experience, and for those who inhabit our world. When we open our hearts and share our thankfulness with those around us, doors open, barriers fall, chasms are bridged, and the landscape of our lives becomes richer and more fertile. And through gratitude and humility, perhaps each of us in our own small way may then contribute to the effort the Greeks hoped for so many years ago—that we might work together "to tame the savageness of man and make gentle the life of this world."

SAVORY STUFFED PIES

*O*h my goodness! These are so delicious they shouldn't be legal to eat! (I guess if you put the poppy seeds on them and went for a drug test you might fail . . .) Legal or not, this is truly great comfort food, folks—dig in!

INGREDIENTS

1 cup chopped cooked chicken breast

$3/4$ cup mashed potatoes (made from a box of instant potatoes)

4 ounces cream cheese, softened

$1/2$ cup frozen mixed vegetables, cooked

2 tablespoons fresh parsley, chopped

$1/2$ teaspoon poultry seasoning

Salt and black pepper

One and a half (14-ounce) packages piecrust or homemade (see page 211)

1 large egg, beaten

Poppy seeds (optional)

- Preheat the oven to 400°F. Lightly grease a baking sheet.

- In a large bowl, stir together the chicken, mashed potatoes, cream cheese, vegetables, parsley, poultry seasoning, and salt and pepper to taste.

- Roll out the piecrust and, using a medium-size biscuit cutter, make individual circles of dough.

- Place about 3 tablespoons of the chicken mixture just below the center of each dough circle.

- Fold the dough over the filling, using a fork to press and seal the edges.

- Arrange the pies on the prepared baking sheet.

- Brush with the egg and, if desired, sprinkle with the poppy seeds.

- Bake for 20 to 25 minutes, until golden brown.

A SWEET LIFE

- - - - - - - - - - - - - - -

New Chapters . . . New Horizons . . . New Possibilities

*S*ingle motherhood is very special in many ways . . . and it's a grueling endurance contest in many others. I settled in with a newborn and established a routine: breastfeeding, building my day around the baby's needs, and embracing the new reality that I was now living for two. It was exciting most of the time, but occasionally I'd bottom out and feel utterly defeated. Sitting up at three o'clock in the morning with a cranky, hungry baby could be a challenge, and whenever I'd stop and look in the mirror I thought seriously about wearing a bag over my head—I was five-foot-four and fifty-five pounds overweight. Ouch.

But I was determined to keep up with everything I'd set in motion. By the end of the summer, I'd started taking Kendel Skye with me everywhere—to the shop, to meetings, to the grocery store—mostly because she wouldn't self-soothe, and she wouldn't let anyone else calm her down with a pacifier or a bottle. When she was about three months old, I had to go to Austin and San Antonio to scout possible locations for some new stores. It would be me, my brother Randall, and Kendel Skye—the three musketeers. It turned into a real trip from hell, and it more or less illustrated what my life was like for about a year.

For starters, we got to the Nashville airport late and had to run for the plane, dragging diaper bags, luggage, and a car seat through the terminal. (Nobody had told me you could rent a car seat at every car rental agency!) Now, August in Tennessee is not a good time to do this—the humidity was about three thousand percent, and I was seriously out of shape. By the time we got to the gate, I was gasping for breath and sweating like a farm animal. We straggled aboard and I perspired all the way to San Antonio while Kendel Skye yelled her head off. (I was clueless about how babies' inner ears can get irritated in pressurized airplane cabins.) A sympathetic flight attendant could see I was still absorbing the truth of what single motherhood was really all about. She suggested I go ahead and feed the baby during takeoff to help relieve the pressure in her ears—a welcome new trick of the trade.

We got to San Antonio at high noon, and (naturally) it was 115 degrees. Randall had arranged for a rental car, but (of course) it turned out to be a tiny, postage-stamp-size subcompact. Kendel Skye and I got into the back, and the air conditioner barely worked. (Perfect!) Randall got behind the wheel and we headed out, bouncing along the streets of ol' San Antone. Immediately, my new daughter let us know just how much she hated the whole thing. She started screaming bloody murder, and it didn't appear that she would stop any-time soon.

After about a half mile Randall peered at me in the rearview mirror.

"Do you think you could maybe shut the kid up for a little while?"

I thought honesty was my best option. "I'm gonna go out on a limb here and say no."

Everything was especially tough because I was completely exhausted. Kendel Skye stuck to a diabolical schedule. Down at 7:00, up at 9:00. Asleep again at 10:00, up at 12:00. Down at 2:30 and then up again at 4:00. Then we'd repeat the whole cycle. I'd grab a few winks here and there, often sitting up in a chair. Not exactly the life of an entrepreneurial, visionary businesswoman that you might read about in *Forbes* magazine.

We raced around San Antonio in our pint-size car, hop-scotching from one possible location to another. We visited empty retail spaces, evaluated traffic conditions, measured prox-imity to other businesses, and tried to get the feel of each area.

Finally, after the fifth or sixth stop, we pulled into a barbecue joint to eat and I hit the wall. Kendel Skye was still crying, and I was pretty sure that after wrestling with her all day I'd developed a hernia. It was Texas-hot and muggy, there were flies all over the place, and I was miserable. I was so tired I couldn't even eat.

That night we made it to Austin, and after I got Kendel Skye changed and bedded down I flopped facedown on the bed and I knew I had somehow pulled a muscle, which—along with my still-unhealed C-section incision—added another layer of pain to the proceedings.

The next day we had fourteen sites to inspect, and I was in no mood for niceties. I just bluntly declared, "Listen, based on how it went yesterday, I'm guessing I've only got about half a dozen stops in me. Pick your top six and let's go see 'em."

We got through the day, chose the sites, and headed for the airport. As I settled into a window seat, I could barely hold my head up. And luckily, the baby was zonked, too. I prayed she'd stay that way for just a couple more hours.

A chipper male flight attendant came by. "Hey, aren't you Gigi . . . the cupcake lady?"

I managed a nod.

"You are so awesome. I just had your cupcakes in Nashville. Are you building a store here?"

I tried to be upbeat. "Yeah." But Kendel Skye started to squawk. I excused myself, and the flight attendant moved off with a smile.

Randall saw me getting ready to feed her and suddenly looked concerned. "You can't pull your boobs out right now!"

"Watch me!" I laughed as the plane pushed back from the gate. I drew a blanket up, unbuttoned, and got Kendel Skye into position. But I couldn't get her latched on. She started twisting and turning. As I struggled with her I could feel my C-section stitches giving way. My pulled muscle howled.

Suddenly the blanket slipped. My boobs popped out and breast milk started shooting all over the seat and into the baby's eyes, which just made her angrier. A guy across the aisle stared at me as we bounced along the taxiway.

Randall freaked. "Good grief, Gigi, cover up!"

He threw a blanket over me as we turned onto the runway, accelerated, and finally climbed up and away from Austin.

After we reached altitude, the flight attendant circled back, surveyed the situation, and saw that Kendel Skye was not settling down. He swept her up in his arms and smiled. "I'm great with babies—check this out."

He walked her up and down the aisle, talking softly to her while passing out pretzels. Within a minute or two, she finally chilled out. I was so grateful I wanted to kiss him. He brought her back, and she latched right on and began feeding peacefully. I clamped my eyes shut and begged God to give me enough strength and patience to get home without losing my mind.

Just then, the flight attendant got on the PA system, welcoming everybody aboard and rattling off information about our travel time. His voice was soothing and familiar, and for the first time in almost two solid days, I leaned back and relaxed.

"You're free to roam around the cabin and use the restroom. I'm also happy to say that we have a special celebrity with us today. Gigi, the genius who founded Gigi's Cupcakes, is sitting in 16-C. If you want to stop by and say hello, I'm sure she'd love to see you."

"Welcome to my new world," I thought, and laughed helplessly.

– – – – –

When Kendel Skye was six months old, I started feeling the need to get back in shape, to shed the excess weight I'd picked up during my pregnancy, and to get myself ready to reenter the world of dating.

A friend took me to Relevé One in Franklin, Tennessee, and turned me on to barre lessons, a brilliant exercise regimen that combines elements of ballet, yoga, and Pilates. It was intimidating at first because I was the heaviest person in the class, but the instructor immediately made me feel welcome. Then she put me through the wringer, and it was hands down the hardest physical workout I had ever done. (I now call it the torture session!)

I started taking class three days a week, rain or shine, sick or well, no matter what was on my schedule, even if it was going to kill me. And I started walking two miles six times a week. And a funny thing happened: I gradually got in shape. I started feeling better and stronger, and the weight came off and stayed off.

I fell in love with both the program and the girls who took classes there. I made lifelong friends at Relevé, encouraging, positive, and godly women. Despite our focus on getting in shape, we all reminded ourselves that developing strength on the inside was just as important. This was just another element of the balance I'd been looking for in my life, and it brought me peace along with better health. I didn't go crazy trying to lose every ounce possible. Did I want to be five pounds lighter? Absolutely. But that would have required me to forget about sweet tea and cupcakes . . . and that was not a trade I was willing to make!

But this routine kept me fit and let me eat what I wanted— within reason. But it could be a struggle. If you don't believe me, try to watch your weight working in a cupcake shop—geez, I might touch a hundred different types of sweets in one day! Being around that kind of temptation all the time was tough.

But I found a technique that helped. I've always loved

watching cooking shows on TV, and I noticed how chefs were constantly messing around with their recipes, tweaking and refining—and tasting everything. It dawned on me that the reason they all don't weigh 600 pounds is that they spit everything out. So I borrowed this little secret and took it into my kitchen. It was hard—I wanted to swallow everything!—but I trained myself to taste what I was cooking or baking without eating it. Another piece of the puzzle—willpower!

– – – – –

By the end of 2009, Gigi's Cupcakes had opened twelve stores. We grew steadily, adding between twelve and twenty-five stores a year. And by the end of 2014, we had nearly a hundred stores.

Around this time, I started to look ahead, and I tried to visualize where all this was taking me. I'd spent the better part of five years running on pure adrenaline, determined to make my dream come true at almost any cost. Now it was finally here in full flower. What had started as a crazy idea was now poised to become the biggest cupcake chain in the world. I don't know if I could have been any prouder of what I'd accomplished, but I also couldn't help thinking of the old Peggy Lee song, "Is That All There Is?".

The truth was, I enjoyed the chase more than anything else. I loved taking a raw concept and bringing it to life through sheer willpower. Don't get me wrong; I wasn't averse to making money or seeing my picture on magazine covers, but I didn't dream up Gigi's just to make money or to become famous. I did it to prove it could be done. And now that I'd reached that goal, I started thinking about what would come next.

I was a single mother with a beautiful baby, and I was finally full of confidence. I now understood that virtually anything I could imagine could come true with enough hard work. And the truth was, I was growing tired of running a big company. I found that I spent most of my time and energy squabbling with employees, wearing myself out on the road, battling with my CFO and the Gigi's business team, and dealing with the demands and criticisms of my vocal and opinionated franchisees.

The most grueling and unsatisfying problems on my desk had to do with the constant needs and demands of my own family members, whom I had gifted with ownership percentages. Having pointedly ignored the old warning against mixing family and business, I now had to deal with the reality that sometimes my own flesh and blood were more focused on making money than they were on enjoying their new, blessed lives.

I decided that while I could certainly run a company and function as a CEO, maybe deep down I didn't really want to. Creativity was my first love and my guiding principle, and I had learned that being a big-shot executive didn't always give me much room to be creative.

So, by 2016, after eight good years of building Gigi's into a national brand, I concluded that I'd personally done everything I could with my original idea. It was time to hand Gigi's off to people who really knew what they were doing, who could take it to the next level. I needed to be a mom, recharge my batteries, and find some real joy.

Our balance sheet looked great, and our financial advisers suggested it was an ideal time to sell the company. An opportunity came along, and we found a buyer. I decided to sell Gigi's but keep my original flagship store in Nashville. I had built a terrific company and felt pride of authorship for sure, but my first love was the Broadway store. The truth was I'd rather be in the kitchen whipping up new recipes than sitting in a boardroom plotting future expansion. It was bittersweet to see ownership of the company pass into someone else's hands, but it was the right business decision. I'd continue to collaborate with Gigi's new owners as founder, spokeswoman, and ribbon cutter/baker's assistant (I still like to get flour all over myself). And it turned out to be great fun—and a source of deep satisfaction—to watch as Gigi's did in fact become the largest cupcake chain in the world.

On the personal front, I began to explore new areas of opportunity. I began speaking to professional and trade groups, universities, and chambers of commerce. I designed a line of properties and products under my new "Gigi" brand label, including cookware, candles, and other home goods, and I went incognito on CBS's *Undercover Boss* TV show, a fun and rewarding experience that got me hooked on the idea of developing my own television properties.

I found real joy and eagerly set my sights on new horizons.

– – – – –

Now that I had a little more time on my hands to think about the future, I found that I could also reflect on the past from a calm and mature perspective.

For instance, I'd long feared that I would never be able to have kids, that maybe God would punish me for not being a better person. But I came to understand that God doesn't work that way. He's full of love and grace, and I'm sure He must have known when I was ready to be a mother, and that any child of mine would be wanted, loved, and cherished.

Who knows what Kendel Skye will make of her life? Not me. But I have some certainty that she'll apprehend the world in her own confident and optimistic way. I hope she'll embrace the things that I can give her that are good—like the self-confidence I had at fifteen to start a business, and the wanderlust and determination that carried me halfway across the country to pursue not one but two lovely dreams. She'll have the benefit of learning from all my bumps and bruises, too. And she'll see the world in a different way than I did—with more hope, I hope.

Like my mother was for me, I'll be behind Kendel Skye no matter what comes. I'll try to avoid second-guessing her, and I'll strive to be patient enough to let her be wrong so she'll ultimately learn from her mistakes. I'll encourage her to dream big like my parents taught me. And she'll live her life knowing that she'll always have at least one dependable person in her corner.

My parents taught me that it's really not all that hard to distinguish right from wrong. I trust Kendel Skye will come to this same realization, and that she'll live her life with honesty, humility, and integrity. I hope she'll be kind to both people and animals, respect the earth, and become the kind of independent woman that I've tried to be.

I'm still a young woman, and God willing, I'll have many more years with my daughter. I hope I'll be there for her when she falls in love, when she marries, and when she brings her own child into the world. I hope to be there to cradle that new life in my arms and welcome another generation aboard.

I'll say, "Hi there, little one. Welcome to the big beautiful world. I've been Gigi for a long time now, and it's been an honor, but you can call me Tootsie."

And then I'll spoil the dickens out of that little kid!

George Bernard Shaw wrote, "Life isn't about finding yourself. Life is about creating yourself." And so I pray that my daughter fearlessly creates herself as her dreams dictate, remaining faithful to God and to her friends, always striving to be respectful and helpful to those around her, weak or strong, rich or poor.

I want her to look back and say, "My mom loved me and taught me things and encouraged me to be who I wanted to be. She taught me how to be kind and loving, to give of myself, and to leave the world a better place than I found it."

That's my "secret ingredient," a legacy of love I want to leave for Kendel Skye—and, if it doesn't sound too self-important, for everyone else whose path I crossed while I was here.

Now that's a sweet life.

- - - - - - - - - -

Lessons for Life and Business

At the midpoint of my time here on earth, I've come to understand a simple, elegant, and uplifting truth that I think we all learn in our own way, in our own time. Our lives may not turn out exactly how we envisioned them, and they may unspool in a fashion wholly different from what we wanted or expected. But this is not cause for disappointment or despair. It's a hallmark of our humanity, and a call for each of us to draw on our strength and creativity to do the best we can with what we're given—for ourselves, for our loved ones, and for the world around us. I believe this is what God expects of us, and what we should expect of ourselves and of one another. For what we will eventually discover is an appreciation of this sweet but ever-challenging life, the quiet contentment that comes with finding a place in the world, and the comforting knowledge that our experiences will guide and inspire our children to find richness and purpose in the years to come. And finally, at the end of our days, what will matter is not what we originally envisioned but what we did with the glorious gifts of life and love and time that He gave us.

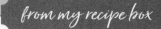
GIGI'S FRIENDSHIP TEA

*Y*ou can always buy a gift at the store, but a homemade gift is something special. During Christmas I usually make a huge batch of this delicious tea mix to give as gifts. You can also add about ¼ cup of this mix to 3 cups water and simmer in a pan on the stove to make your home smell of spice, love, and goodness!

INGREDIENTS

I quart Tang

I quart lemonade made from a mix

I cup Lipton instant tea powder

¹/₂ cup sugar

I tablespoon ground cinnamon

2 teaspoons ground allspice

2 teaspoons ground cloves

I teaspoon ground ginger

¹/₄ cup Red Hot candies

- In a large bowl, mix together the Tang, lemonade, instant tea, and sugar.

- Add the spices and Red Hot candies.

- Store in jars.

- To serve, add 2½ teaspoons tea mix to a cup of hot water and stir.

ACKNOWLEDGMENTS

I believe gratitude is one of the most important secret ingredients a person can add to the mix as they create a full and successful life.

A long time ago I started keeping a "gratitude journal," in which I chronicled various stories and reminders of the people who helped me along the way. I found that jotting a few thoughts down whenever I felt lost or discouraged kept me focused on what really mattered in this life. I learned that a heart that is grateful is also light and free—and open to seeing new possibilities that might otherwise be overlooked when the modern world is occasionally fogged over by uncertainty, challenge, or doubt.

When I sat down to write this book, I'd already been blessed by years of support and affection from my friends and loved ones. Although it would probably take a whole *other* book to list them all, I do want to single out a handful whose generosity and constancy have made my life richer and happier.

I owe my warmest thanks to . . .

My beautiful daughter, Kendel Skye, who teaches me something new every day. Lynn Woodall, who makes my trains run on time and solves every problem that comes over the transom—thank you for being a part of my life and helping me find balance and order each day. Marc, Maya, and Morgan Wank, my "second family." My cousin and friend Amanda Cox, whom I greatly admire. My sweet aunts Bennie, Patty, Diane, Nancy, and Sharon. Mark and Vivian Ericson, Buster and Darlene Wolfe, Susan Snowdon and her amazing son, Michael, and Candice Benward, whose massage therapy has kept me upright and glowing through years of gigs, house cleanings, and cupcake shop openings. Bobby and Cindy Harrington, Josh and Joni Patrick, and the Cain family—thank you for your spiritual guidance and prayers. My two sweet nieces, Ali Butler and Emilyn Bell. To my faith family, and all of my dear friends who have guided me through good times and hard times. And much love and appreciation to my stalwart and true comrades Brittney Swafford and Heather Frey, who lead the incredible team at my original Gigi's flagship store on Broadway in downtown Nashville.

I've been blessed to have some truly great professionals in my corner this last year. Attorney and manager Wayne Halper took command of my far-flung interests and set the table for many wonderful opportunities, including this book. My cowriter, Bud Schaetzle, was devoted to capturing what was in my head and heart, and to putting it all to work with honesty and taste. Melissa and Rick Caballo at Dead Horse Branding brought a breath of much-needed fresh air into my creative life.

And David Larabell at CAA was behind me from day one, his good counsel informing every step I've taken.

A special thank-you to Jonathan Merkh, Philis Boulting-house, and Becky Nesbitt at Howard Books, who welcomed me into the Simon & Schuster family and showed me possibilities I'd never dreamed of. As I worked on this project, I became convinced that their confidence in me and support for this book came straight out of the book of Hebrews, which reminds us that "faith is the substance of things hoped for, the evidence of things not seen."

And finally, to all the delightful people I've encountered over the years who came out to hear me sing, hired me to keep their homes beautiful, and took a chance on my cupcakes, God bless you all for helping to bring meaning, joy, and purpose into my life.

Gigi

FRANKLIN, TENNESSEE

RECIPE INDEX

INDEX